AF891630

Money Smartly

What They Forgot To Teach You

Jeremy Verbit

Money Smartly

Copyright © 2018 by Jeremy Verbit

ISBN-13 978-0-578-44606-6

ISBN-10 0-578-44606-5

All rights reserved. No part of this publication may be reproduced, scanned, or transmitted in any form, digital or printed, without the written permission of the author.

www.MoneySmartly.com

~

To my wife Stephanie for her support,

To my mom and dad for their encouragement,

To my family and friends for their help,

To the ChooseFI community for their direction,

And for all who just want to be able to manage their money smartly without doing enough research to warrant a PhD.

~

Preface

Growing up, school taught us the skills necessary to get a job and make money. But they forgot to teach us the best ways to put that money to use! Not once did a teacher or professor I had review budgeting, projecting finances, bank account buffers, defined contribution plans such as 401(k)s, credit, credit cards, emergency funds, IRAs, taxable accounts, health insurance, 529s, car loans, student loans, mortgages, life insurance, car insurance, homeowners and renters insurance, taxes, or retirement planning. Chances are every one of those topics applies to you over your lifetime. How well you leverage each one directly influences your net worth, flexibility, and freedom all while being, generally speaking, more under your control than your income. I wrote Money Smartly to share how you can take advantage of these vehicles to optimize your net worth while keeping your funds sufficiently liquid. I wrote Money Smartly to improve lives.

Money Smartly is certainly not the only resource picking up where schools left off on personal finance education. A number of personal finance authors have cropped up over the years with advice; however, the most popular resources are lacking in actionable and sound advice backed up by demonstrative evidence. For example, Suze Orman's best-selling book "The Money Book for the Young, Fabulous & Broke" offers great advice for what types of accounts to put your money in, but doesn't complete the advice with what funds to invest your money in and why, leaving the reader questioning how to follow through with the advice. Dave Ramsey's "The Total Money Makeover" provides good encouragement for eliminating debt, but no readers maximize their wealth by paying off low interest, small loans before high interest, large loans as he suggests doing.[1] Money Smartly presents the tools available for you to optimize your net worth while keeping your funds sufficiently liquid and demonstrates *how* and just as importantly *why* to use those tools. It walks you through making a personal plan for *your* money and monitoring that plan. It allows you to modify your plan—and recognize the resulting consequences—if you find it limits your spending too much for your liking. By the end of this book, you will be able to use these tools to craft a personal plan that works for you now and all the way through retirement.

---

[1] https://www.nerdwallet.com/blog/credit-cards/dave-ramsey-credit-cards/

Who Money Smartly Was Written For

Readers who are actively working private or public employees, whether in your early 20s or late 60s, will get the most out of Money Smartly. Its content still applies for self-employed readers, but doesn't review self-employed retirement accounts or tax strategies. It also applies to retired readers, but its advice focuses more heavily on how to prepare for wealth drawdown in retirement than how to adjust your spending throughout retirement. Moreover, Money Smartly focuses on how to best put the money you earn to use rather than discussing strategies to increase your income or climb the corporate ladder.

References

Money Smartly was built from about a decade of researching a plethora of articles, academic papers, and books with a vast variety of recommendations, many good and many more bad. My goal was to piece together the best advice in one place and spare you the bad advice to provide a one-stop shop of condensed solid financial advice. While I present the advice necessary to manage your money optimally and the supporting evidence to understand why it works, if you are looking to read more in depth on any particular topic, I recommend following up with the works I cite alongside the content in the footnotes or endnotes (depending on the format of Money Smartly you have).

Throughout Money Smartly we'll cover specific companies that offer superior services. While I use these services myself, I have no association with the companies nor benefit financially from recommending them in this book. I use them because I believe in them and I recommend them because I want you to benefit from them as well.

Money Smartly Priorities

The most common question regarding money is where to put your money to use first. Should you build an emergency fund in a checking account or fund a Roth IRA? Should you pay down student loan debt or invest? Should you fund an HSA or a 401(k)? As we progress through Money Smartly we will be building an ordered list of financial priorities summarized at the end of each chapter and as your financial situation improves or you earn more disposable income you can move on to the next financial priority. For that reason, Money Smartly is designed to be read from front to back. Chapters are arranged such that if you are interested in a particular topic you can jump directly to the corresponding chapter, but be aware the chapter may assume an understanding of or point to knowledge from a previous chapter.

Table of Contents

Chapter 1 – Why Do You Want Money?

Why do you want money?! To most people that sounds like a pretty silly question: we want money to buy things! The truth is people want money for different reasons and for different times of their lives. Some want to save for a wedding, buy a house, get a degree, save for children, go on a vacation, pursue a hobby, take a sabbatical, semi-retire, or retire early. It's worth remembering that your money is only as good as the happiness it buys you. There are many paths to happiness that don't require money, but we're here to help you unlock the paths that do. You don't need to know all your paths to make a plan for your money, but if you do have particular goals in mind, it's important to include those in your plan.

For most people I've met, after they've built up the money for their shorter term goals the primary reason to acquire money is for the freedom it provides. A Gallup poll found that in 2015, 68% of workers were not engaged in their job and that number has been relatively consistent at least since 2011.[2] It's no wonder why people are looking to acquire enough money to retire early or find a more satisfying albeit lower paying job, often referred to as "semi-retirement." Even if you aren't looking to retire early, reaching a point of "financial independence" where you no longer rely on your job and are in a position to negotiate working on your own terms can reap major benefits to your happiness. The only way to build a nest-egg capable of supporting your financial independence is to earn more money than you spend and invest the difference.

How much money do you need to have saved before you can safely retire? This question has been answered by a reputable study by three professors of finance at Trinity University called the Trinity Study.[3] It says that you can withdraw 4%, increased yearly with inflation, of your nest-egg each year and have a greater than 96% chance of your nest-egg lasting at least 30 years. If you're looking for a much longer retirement of 40+ years, the safe withdrawal rate falls down to as low as 3.5%, the point at which your nest-

---

[2] http://www.gallup.com/poll/188144/employee-engagement-stagnant-2015.aspx
[3] http://afcpe.org/assets/pdf/vol1014.pdf

egg is almost certain to sustain itself indefinitely.[4] This means that once you've acquired 1/0.035 or about 29 times your yearly expenses you can retire at any age and be confident you won't outlive your savings because the return they'll generate in investments have become a "perpetual money-making machine" generating enough income to cover your expenses forever.

How long it takes you to save 29 times your yearly expenses comes down to what percentage of your yearly income you save. At one extreme, if you save 100% of your income then you have no expenses and can retire today never needing nor spending money. At the other extreme, if you save 0% of your income then you aren't increasing your nest-egg and can never retire without the help of a pension or social security. Each additional percentage point of your income you save can bring you years closer to retirement.

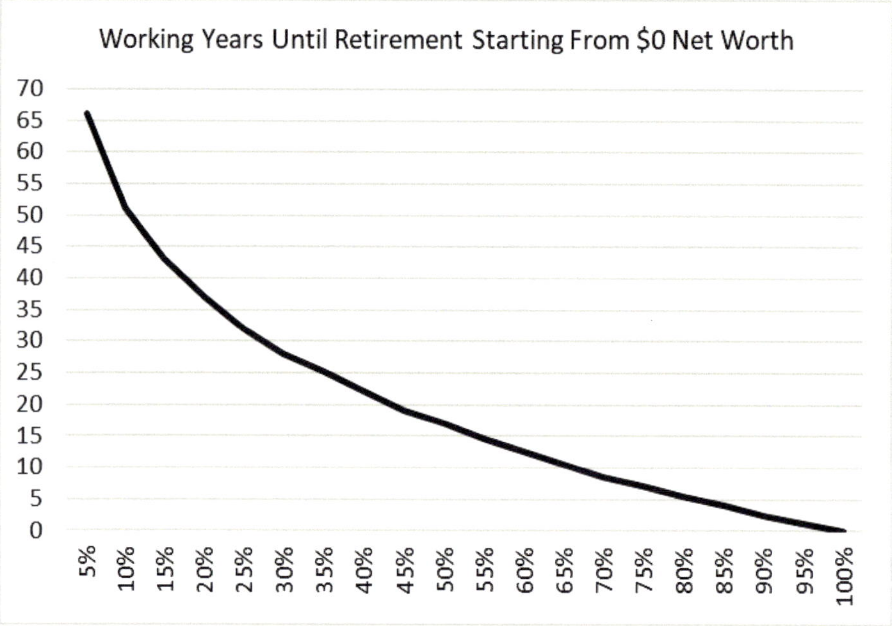

[4]https://www.kitces.com/blog/adjusting-safe-withdrawal-rates-to-the-retirees-time-horizon/

If you love your job and intend to work for the rest of your life, maybe you're looking to increase your nest-egg to leave as an inheritance to your loved ones. Or maybe you're just looking to get your financial house in order. Whatever your goals, short-term or long, money plays a role and Money Smartly will help you develop a plan for your goals.

Chapter 2 – Budgeting

Knowing how you spend your money is the most fundamental element of personal finance. It's necessary to ensure you spend less than you earn and to project what your financial situation will look like in the future. This ability to forecast your finances will enable you to adjust your financial plan to meet your goals and determine which tools you can leverage to your advantage. It's for these reasons that we start our journey outlining proper budgeting.

Most people approach budgeting like they do dieting: "For the next several months I will cut my calories to a minimum until I reach my desired weight." Similarly with budgeting, they cut discretionary spending to a minimum leaving themselves starved of any fun. Again, money is only as good as the happiness it buys you. The problem is that too often people buy a little happiness now at the expense of more happiness later without knowing what they're sacrificing. If you knew that monthly cable bill would cost you four additional working years before reaching financial independence, would you think twice about renewing it? Some would, some wouldn't. The key is having the information to assess the future consequences of your purchases by forecasting your finances. Budgets act as guardrails to keep your spending from diverging from your priorities.

The classic approach to budgeting is to estimate how much you plan to spend on particular categories then track your spending against that plan. Many use their banks' websites to track their spending but this either limits them to using one bank for all their accounts or requires them to manually aggregate their spending across the many banks they use. This hassle alone has kept many from tracking their spending. Luckily, tracking that spending has become much easier over the last decade thanks to new technology.

The best way to track your spending is using an online aggregated personal finance manager such as Mint.com or PersonalCapital.com. These sites allow you to sync your bank accounts, credit cards, loans, and investment accounts to them to automatically track your spending against your planned budgets. You'll need to use credit or debit cards for your expenses to enable these personal finance managers to automatically track your spending, but as we'll see in Chapter 7 – Credit Cards, this practice comes with rewards.

Syncing Your Accounts

Mint.com is my favorite online aggregated personal finance manager because it's free, designed first and foremost to track your spending against your budgets, and is easy to use; therefore, we'll use it for our walkthrough but the process is similar for PersonalCapital.com and other aggregators.

Your first step to track your spending with Mint is to sign up and sync your external accounts. You'll need to have setup online access to each external account you sync to Mint including each bank, credit card company, and loan servicing company you work with. Once you have an online account with these companies, you can search those companies by name or web URL on Mint and use the username and password you setup with those companies to sync your external accounts to your Mint account.

Once synced, these accounts will automatically update Mint about any transactions in those accounts, including the establishment, category, and amount of those transactions. This isn't only useful for tracking expenses, but also for monitoring for fraudulent transactions. I have had numerous occasions where Mint has saved me hundreds of dollars by bringing to my attention a purchase I did not make and the credit card company did not flag as fraudulent until I notified them.

Building Budgets

The next step is to build your budgets by category. This will enable you to track where your money is going and ensure you are not overspending your budgets each month. If you have created a budget for all your expenses before, this will be easy. If you haven't, you should start by estimating how much you spend per month on each of the following categories:

- Auto & Transport
    - Auto Insurance

- Auto Payment
- Gas & Fuel
- Parking
- Public Transportation

- Bills & Utilities
  - Electric Bill
  - Gas Bill
  - Phone
  - Internet
  - Television
- Education
  - Student Loan
- Entertainment
  - Alcohol
  - Venues
- Food & Dining
  - Groceries
  - Restaurants
- Health & Fitness
  - Gym
  - Supplements
- Home
  - Rent/Mortgage
  - Homeowners/Renters Insurance (if paid monthly or more frequently)
  - Homeowners Association Fees (if paid monthly or more frequently)
  - Home Services (if paid monthly or more frequently)
- Pets
  - Food
  - Supplies
- Other Miscellaneous Expenses
  - Shopping
  - Gifts & Donations
  - Travel
  - Property Taxes
  - Haircuts
  - Books & Supplies

- Tuition

I recommend setting a budget for each of the high level bullet points that apply to you. You don't want to set your budgets too finely—such as for each of the indented bullet points—because that will leave you less flexibility to shift budget from one subcategory to another. One example of this is a commuter deciding to take public transport instead of driving to work, adding spending to Public Transport but removing it from Gas & Fuel and Parking. Your goal is to make sure the high level areas of your life stay under budget and if they don't, you know you either need to make a plan to reduce your spending in that area or increase your budget and accept the consequences that has on your savings. Don't worry about estimating your budgets too precisely: we will use the spending we track in Mint to adjust your budgets over time. In Chapter 3 – Projecting Finances, we will go over how to see the short term impact and the long term impact of increasing or decreasing your budget.

All irregular spending that requires a timeline of more than a month to analyze its trend because it will be large one month and small or nonexistent another month should fall under the Other Miscellaneous Expenses category. You should try to estimate your average monthly expenditure for this category and set that as your budget. The budget for this category will probably need the most adjusting as you track your spending against it. You can overspend your budget on Other Miscellaneous Expenses in a given month, but each quarter you should reassess your monthly expenditure and adjust your budget accordingly or if your spending is too high, plan ways to reduce it in some of the subcategories. Just because you aren't setting budgets on subcategories doesn't mean you can't review your spending habits in those subcategories. Mint's "Trends" feature provides a very easy way to review your spending trends in any category or subcategory over any period of time.

Just like with the Other Miscellaneous Expenses category, you should review your spending for all other categories and adjust your budgets or plan ways to reduce your spending if you end up over budget, but you should review these categories just after the end of each month. You should also review each transaction over that month to ensure the transaction was categorized correctly. Although Mint automatically categorizes most transactions correctly, there will usually be a few transactions that you'll need to correct. A common example is purchases in a gas station's convenience store being categorized as "Gas & Fuel" when they are actually "Groceries." In Mint, you can correct these by clicking the category of the transaction and selecting a new category from the dropdown list. You can also click "Edit Details" and check "Always rename and categorize as <the selected category name>" which will tell Mint to set any future purchase from this establishment into the selected category automatically moving forward.

Your account transfers that debit one account and credit another account (such as debiting your checking account and crediting your credit card account for a credit card payment) should fall into a category that doesn't need a budget since this is just transferring money and isn't an expense. In Mint, these will fall under the "Transfer" category automatically. A similar scenario happens if you are being reimbursed for expenses, which is often the case for work-related travel. I recommend setting up a new "Paid Travel" category for these expenses. In Mint, you can create a new category in the same dropdown you used to override categories for transactions.

Notifications

You should setup notifications to email you when you exceed your budgets to help you recognize when you need to slow your spending for the month. Mint allows a variety of notifications including the following with the most useful ones bolded:

- Bill Reminder Alerts
  - Nice to have, but these won't be necessary once we set these on autopay in Chapter 7 – Credit Cards.
- Spending Alerts
  - **Low Balance** – Will alert you if any checking or savings account balance falls below a dollar threshold you set.
    - Useful if any checking or savings account you use has a minimum balance or overdraft fees.
  - Low Credit Availability – Will alert you if your credit availability drops below a dollar threshold you set.
  - Total Credit Available – Will alert you if your credit availability is low enough to hurt your credit score.

- **Unusual Spending** – Will alert you if you're spending much more in any category than you typically do.
  - Useful to monitor for fraudulent transactions.
- **Overbudget** – Will alert you if you go over one of your category budgets.
  - This is the most useful notification of them all.
- Interest Rate – Will alert you if the interest rate on one of your credit cards or loans changes.
- Trade Commissions – Will alert you if you're charged trade commissions on your investment accounts.
- **Bank Fees** – Will alert you if you are charged bank fees above a dollar threshold you set.
  - Useful because banks aren't always straightforward with their fees and if you are being charged any significant amount of fees you should change banks.
  - Sometimes you can ask your bank to credit back these fees when you catch them.
- Large Purchases – Will alert you if there are any purchases above a dollar threshold you set.
- Large Deposit – Will alert you when a deposit above a dollar threshold you set clears and is available.
- Auto Insurance Spending – Will alert you when you are spending too much on auto insurance.
- Health Insurance Spending -Will alert you when you are spending too much on health insurance.
- Home & Mortgage Notifications – Will alert you when you are spending too much on your mortgage.
- 401k Roller – Will alert you when you have a 401k rollover.
- Goal Notifications – Will alert you when goal milestones, which you can set, are met and these notifications also provide monthly updates.

Financial Priorities

1. **Automate expense tracking and establish categorized budgets to control and predict your spending.**

Chapter 3 – Projecting Finances

While budgeting makes your expenses predictable, projections make your accounts predictable. Like a crystal ball, financial projections enable you to simulate scenarios to see their impact on your future financial situation. Whereas budgets tell you *what* you can spend, projections tell you *when* you can spend. They tell you when you can buy a car, buy a house, afford your wedding, go on a vacation or retire all without fear of resulting financial troubles in the future. The sole reason anyone experiences money shortfalls is because they didn't see them early enough to prevent them.

A key tenant to projecting your finances is that your method be flexible because your income, expenses, and accounts will change over your lifetime. I prefer to project my finances in a Microsoft Excel spreadsheet because it's simple to use and flexible. Your projections should match the period of your budgets and so creating a timeline with each row reflecting a month is appropriate. Start with the current month and label each consecutive month down the spreadsheet row by row through at least five years into the future, but there's no reason you couldn't go longer. Each column should represent a category of income, expenses, an account transfer, or an account balance. Account transfer columns are the monthly amounts you contribute towards paying credit cards, paying loans, or investing in investment accounts. Monthly income, expenses, and account transfers all add or remove money from the previous month's account balances. It's the account balances that you're looking to predict in the future and we'll help you spot worrisome balances throughout Money Smartly.

For now, we'll focus on establishing and updating your projections from estimates to actualities after each month ends. Creating your projections for the first time may take a few hours and is perhaps the most onerous exercise in Money Smartly. After that, updating your projections to reflect actual income, expenses, account transfers, and account balances as each month closes should take less than ten minutes at the start of each month.

The rest of your financial plan will be set on autopilot after establishment and these ten minutes each month are all you'll need to ensure you stay your course.

Building Your Projections Spreadsheet

Your projection spreadsheet should look similar to the figure below. Let's walk through each column, then you can setup your own spreadsheet using the figure below as your guide and modify it to fit your income, expenses, and accounts. If any accounts are unfamiliar to you, you can skip them for now and we'll go over them in later chapters.

	Income					Expenses		Account Transfers: Debits				Account Transfers: Credits			
	% Stocks	Job	Additional Income	401k Match	HSA Match	Budgeted Expenses	Additional Expenses	Credit Cards	Student Loans	Auto Loans	Home Loan	401k	Roth IRA	Taxable	HSA
Int. Rate:	-	-	-	-	-	-	-	-	-	-	-	-	-	-	-
Jan-17	90%	$3,400	$0	$100	$25	$1,400	$0	$250	$150	$250	$700	$100	$458	$10	$25
Feb-17	90%	$3,400	$0	$100	$25	$1,400	$0	$250	$150	$250	$700	$100	$458	$10	$25
Mar-17	90%	$3,400	$800	$100	$25	$1,400	$300	$250	$150	$250	$700	$100	$458	$10	$25
Apr-17	90%	$3,400	$0	$100	$25	$1,400	$0	$250	$150	$250	$700	$100	$458	$10	$25
May-17	90%	$3,400	$0	$100	$25	$1,400	$0	$250	$150	$250	$700	$100	$458	$10	$25
Jun-17	90%	$3,400	$800	$100	$25	$1,400	$1,800	$250	$150	$250	$700	$100	$458	$10	$25
Jul-17	90%	$3,400	$0	$100	$25	$1,400	$0	$250	$150	$250	$700	$100	$458	$10	$25
Aug-17	90%	$3,400	$0	$100	$25	$1,400	$0	$250	$150	$250	$700	$100	$458	$10	$25
Sep-17	90%	$3,400	$800	$100	$25	$1,400	$300	$250	$150	$250	$700	$100	$458	$10	$25
Oct-17	90%	$3,400	$0	$100	$25	$1,400	$0	$250	$150	$250	$700	$100	$458	$10	$25
Nov-17	90%	$3,400	$0	$100	$25	$1,400	$0	$250	$150	$250	$700	$100	$458	$10	$25
Dec-17	90%	$3,400	$800	$100	$25	$1,400	$1,800	$250	$150	$250	$700	$100	$458	$10	$25

	Account Balances: Liabilities				Account Balances: Assets				Home	Cash	Net Worth	Notes
	Credit Cards	Student Loans	Auto Loans	Home Loan	401k	Roth IRA	Taxable	HSA	Home	Checking	Net Worth	Notes
Int. Rate:	15.0%	6.5%	3.0%	4.5%	N/A	N/A	N/A	N/A	2.0%	1.0%	-	-
Jan-17	$5,000	$20,000	$10,000	$140,000	$5,000	$5,000	$10	$50	$140,000	$3,500	-$21,440	
Feb-17	$4,810	$19,958	$9,774	$139,823	$5,130	$5,490	$20	$101	$140,234	$3,560	-$19,831	
Mar-17	$4,617	$19,915	$9,548	$139,646	$5,261	$5,983	$30	$151	$140,467	$4,120	-$17,713	
Apr-17	$4,422	$19,873	$9,322	$139,468	$5,392	$6,479	$41	$203	$140,702	$4,181	-$16,087	
May-17	$4,225	$19,830	$9,094	$139,289	$5,525	$6,978	$51	$254	$140,936	$4,241	-$14,452	
Jun-17	$4,025	$19,787	$8,866	$139,110	$5,658	$7,480	$61	$306	$141,172	$3,301	-$13,810	
Jul-17	$3,822	$19,743	$8,638	$138,930	$5,792	$7,985	$72	$358	$141,407	$3,361	-$12,159	
Aug-17	$3,617	$19,700	$8,409	$138,749	$5,927	$8,492	$82	$410	$141,643	$3,421	-$10,500	
Sep-17	$3,409	$19,656	$8,179	$138,568	$6,062	$9,003	$93	$463	$141,879	$3,981	-$8,331	
Oct-17	$3,199	$19,612	$7,949	$138,386	$6,198	$9,517	$103	$516	$142,116	$4,041	-$6,654	
Nov-17	$2,986	$19,568	$7,718	$138,203	$6,336	$10,034	$114	$570	$142,353	$4,102	-$4,968	
Dec-17	$2,771	$19,523	$7,487	$138,020	$6,473	$10,553	$125	$623	$142,590	$3,162	-$4,274	

Note: You can download this projections spreadsheet template at MoneySmartly.com

Income

- Job
  - This represents the monthly income you expect from your job after taxes. You should include any savings taken out of your income such as contributions to a 401(k).
- Additional Income
  - This represents the amount of money you can expect from any bonuses, tax refunds, etc. I recommend only entering the minimum bonus you can expect for future months. Some prefer to assume they will not receive bonuses in the future and only fill out this column once they actually receive their bonus. This ensures that your projections are conservative and you don't wind up missing money your projections caused you to rely on.
- 401k Match
  - This represents any money added to your 401(k) by your employer. If your employer doesn't contribute to your 401(k), you can skip this column. Oftentimes your employer will match a certain percentage of what you contribute. In these cases, I'd recommend setting the 401k Match column to be calculated as a formula based off your Account Transfers →401k column.
- HSA Match
  - This represents any money added to your HSA by your employer. If your employer doesn't contribute to your HSA, you can skip this column. Oftentimes your employer will match a certain percentage of what you contribute. In these cases, I'd recommend setting the HSA Match column to be calculated as a formula based off your Account Transfers → HSA column.

Expenses

- Budgeted Expenses
  - This represents your estimated monthly expenses including any 'Other Miscellaneous Expenses' you budgeted in your online aggregated personal finance manager you setup in Chapter 2 – Budgeting.
- Additional Expenses

  - This is any additional irregular expenses you incur. An example is a month in which you plan to travel for a vacation, pay auto or homeowners or life insurance, or pay property or additional income taxes. In the future you might want to separate these expenses into a column for each type of expense, but to start it's easiest to group these into one column.

Account Transfers

- Credit Cards
  - This represents the money you plan to use monthly to pay off your credit card balances. If you are paying your credit card balances completely each month, you can keep this column (and your Credit Cards account balance) at $0 because you are simply delaying a cash payment for your expenses for only a month.
- Student Loans
  - This represents the money you plan to use monthly to pay off your student loan balances.
- Auto Loans
  - This represents the money you plan to use monthly to pay off your auto loans.
- Home Loan
  - This represents the money you plan to use to pay off your home loan.
- 401k
  - This represents the money you plan to contribute monthly to your 401(k). Note that because 401(k) contributions come out of your paycheck before taxes, contributions to a 401(k) will increase your "Job" income column due to having less taxes removed from your paycheck.
- Roth IRA
  - This represents the money you plan to contribute monthly to your Roth IRA.
- Taxable
  - This represents the money you plan to contribute monthly to your taxable investment account.
- HSA

  - This represents the money you plan to contribute monthly to your Health Savings Account.

Account Balances

Account balance columns should be setup as formulas starting with that account's previous month's balance and subtracting, for liabilities, or adding, for assets, the associated account transfer. A few accounts will increase from income. For example, your "Checking" account balance is increased by your "Job" and "Bonus" income. Similarly, your "401k" account balance would be increased by your "401k Match" income. On the other hand, your "Checking" account balance will decrease from all expenses and account transfers.

- Liability Accounts
  - Credit Cards
    - This represents the balance of your credit cards at the end of the month.
    - Formula
      - [This Account's Balance for the Previous Month] – [This Month's Credit Card Account Transfer]
  - Student Loans
    - This represents the balance of your student loans at the end of the month.
    - Formula
      - [This Account's Balance for the Previous Month] – [This Month's Student Loan Account Transfer]
  - Auto Loans
    - This represents the balance of your auto loans at the end of the month.
    - Formula
      - [This Account's Balance for the Previous Month] – [This Month's Auto Loan Account Transfer]
  - Home Loan
    - This represents the balance of your mortgage at the end of the month.
    - Formula

            - [This Account's Balance for the Previous Month] – [This Month's Home Loan Account Transfer]

- Asset Accounts
    - 401k
        - This represents the balance of your 401(k) at the end of the month.
        - Formula
            - [This Account's Balance for the Previous Month] + [This Month's 401k Match Income] + [This Month's 401k Account Transfer]
    - Roth IRA
        - This represents the balance of your Roth IRA at the end of the month.
        - Formula
            - [This Account's Balance for the Previous Month] + [This Month's Roth IRA Account Transfer]
    - Taxable
        - This represents the balance of your taxable investment account at the end of the month.
        - Formula
            - [This Account's Balance for the Previous Month] + [This Month's Taxable Account Transfer]
    - HSA
        - This represents the balance of your Health Savings Account at the end of the month.
        - Formula
            - [This Account's Balance for the Previous Month] + [This Month's HSA Account Transfer]
- Home
    - Home
        - This represents the value of your home at the end of the month.
        - Formula
            - [This Account's Balance for the Previous Month]
- Cash Accounts
    - Checking
        - This represents the balance of your checking account at the end of the month.
        - Formula

        - [This Account's Balance for the Previous Month] + [This Month's Income] – [This Month's Expenses] – [This Month's Account Transfers]
- Net Worth
    - This is what you'll be looking to increase over time.
    - Formula:
        - [Cash Account Balances] + [Asset Account Balances] – [Liability Account Balances]

Notes

- Notes
    - This is the place to add notes about any changes to your spending habits. Examples include months you'll start increasing or decreasing your normal monthly account transfers, months you'll have Additional Income or Additional Expenses, or months you expect to reach particular financial goals. These notes will help you remember why these changes occurred.

Impact of Interest Rates on Account Balance Projections

Almost all account balances grow over time due to an interest rate. That's because money available now is worth more than the same amount available in the future due to its potential earning capacity over that time. This is known as "the time value of money." Banks pay you interest to handle your money with savings accounts because you give them cash to hand out in higher interest loans; conversely, banks charge you interest to take their money with credit cards because you cause them to have less cash to hand out in other loans. Any party that can borrow some money to put it to work earning them more money has an interest in doing so.

So far, we haven't incorporated interest rates into our account balance projections because interest rates are a bit complicated and they usually have minor impact over the short to medium term, which is the timeframe your financial projections are primarily forecasting. You don't need to incorporate interest rates to get benefit from your projections. However, we'll walk you through how to incorporate them in case you want to forecast your projections far into the future, such as more than five years from now. Unless you're looking to project the timing of a long-term goal such as retirement, you might prefer to skip straight to the next chapter and avoid the more complicated Excel formulas.

First, if you have multiple credit cards, you'll need to split your "Credit Cards" account balance column into a separate column for each card to account for their different interest rates. Likewise, you'll need to do the same for each student loan and each auto loan. Your 401k, Roth IRA, taxable investment, and HSA interest rates are not fixed and depend on investment returns; therefore, you will need to assume a reasonable expected return based on historical returns.

While historically stocks yielded 10% returns, this is based on ten-year U.S. treasury bonds yielding 5.5% return with very little risk. These treasury bonds are IOUs where you lend the U.S. government money in return for their—very safe—promise to pay you back with a little interest at a future date (in this case in ten years). With an option for such a safe 5.5% return, your riskier stocks needed to yield a premium of about 4.5% on top of treasury bonds in order for investors to justify taking on the increased market risk.[5] However as of September 2018, ten-year U.S. treasury bonds only yield about a 3% return.[6] This means we can expect about a 3% return for typical intermediate-term treasury bonds and a 7.5% return for stocks. This is a very rudimentary means to estimate returns but it will work for our purposes. To simplify handling these investment accounts, rather than splitting each account into a column for stocks and a column for bonds, you can keep each account as a single column and calculate a weighted return, which we'll cover when we review the formulas for returns.

You should insert a row into your spreadsheet below the name of each column and above the first month of your projections and label it "Interest Rate" where you'd typically put the month label. This row will hold the interest rate of each account balance. For each month besides the first month of each account balance, you will enter a formula that incorporates these interest rates. This formula includes the "Account Balance" formula

---

[5] https://blog.wealthfront.com/us-stock-long-term-returns/

[6] https://www.treasury.gov/resource-center/data-chart-center/interest-rates/Pages/TextView.aspx?data=yieldYear&year=2018

we reviewed previously, but multiplies it by a function that accounts for its exponential growth/shrinkage. For example, if you put an interest rate for your credit card in cell N4, your second month's (cell N6) credit card rate projection formula would be:

= ([Account Balance Formula]) * EXP([Account Interest Rate] * (30/360))

= ([Last Month's Credit Card Account Balance] – [This Month's Credit Card Account Transfer]) * EXP([Credit Card Interest Rate] * (30/360))

Or from the example spreadsheet given in the image previously:

= (N5-I6) * EXP(**N4** * (30/360))

You can then drag the formula down the column for each month and have each month be accurate since the dollar signs in N4 keep the formula statically locked on the interest rate cell. The "30" represents the ~30 days between credit card payment in a month and the "360" represents the ~360 days in a year. This formula represents how most accounts compound interest over a presumed 30-day month and 12-month year. Any attempt to get more accurate than this will have negligible impact on your projections.

You should insert a column into your spreadsheet to the right of the month column and label it "% Stocks". For each month you'll put your target percent allocation to stocks. You'll use this to calculate the exponential growth of your investment accounts. For example, your investment accounts can be expected to grow by 3% for bonds and 7.5% for stocks, so you'd enter:

= ([Account Balance Formula]) * EXP((0.075*[This Month's % Stock Allocation] + 0.03*(1 – [This Month's % Stock Allocation])) * 30/360)

Your home, not consisting of stocks or bonds, is probably best to consider as growing with inflation at about 2% using the "Interest Rate" row unless you have a better historical growth rate for your area.

	Q	U	Y	Z
2	**Liabilities**	**Assets**	**Home**	**Cash**
3	Credit Cards	401k	Home	Checking
4	15.0%	N/A	2.0%	1.0%
5	$5,000	$5,000	$140,000	$3,500
6	=(Q5-I6)*EXP(Q4*(30/360))	=(U5+M6)*EXP((B6*0.075+(1-B6)*0.03)*(30/360))	=(Y5)*EXP(Y4*(30/360))	=(Z5+C6+D6-G6-H6-I6-J6-K6-L6-M6-N6-O6-P6)*EXP(Z4*(30/360))
7	=(Q6-I7)*EXP(Q4*(30/360))	=(U6+M7)*EXP((B7*0.075+(1-B7)*0.03)*(30/360))	=(Y6)*EXP(Y4*(30/360))	=(Z6+C7+D7-G7-H7-I7-J7-K7-L7-M7-N7-O7-P7)*EXP(Z4*(30/360))
8	=(Q7-I8)*EXP(Q4*(30/360))	=(U7+M8)*EXP((B8*0.075+(1-B8)*0.03)*(30/360))	=(Y7)*EXP(Y4*(30/360))	=(Z7+C8+D8-G8-H8-I8-J8-K8-L8-M8-N8-O8-P8)*EXP(Z4*(30/360))
9	=(Q8-I9)*EXP(Q4*(30/360))	=(U8+M9)*EXP((B9*0.075+(1-B9)*0.03)*(30/360))	=(Y8)*EXP(Y4*(30/360))	=(Z8+C9+D9-G9-H9-I9-J9-K9-L9-M9-N9-O9-P9)*EXP(Z4*(30/360))
10	=(Q9-I10)*EXP(Q4*(30/360	=(U9+M10)*EXP((B10*0.075+(1-B10)*0.03)*(30/3	=(Y9)*EXP(Y4*(30/360))	=(Z9+C10+D10-G10-H10-I10-J10-K10-L10-M10-N10-O10-P10)*EXP($
11	=(Q10-I11)*EXP(Q4*(30/36	=(U10+M11)*EXP((B11*0.075+(1-B11)*0.03)*(30/	=(Y10)*EXP(Y4*(30/360	=(Z10+C11+D11-G11-H11-I11-J11-K11-L11-M11-N11-O11-P11)*EXP(
12	=(Q11-I12)*EXP(Q4*(30/36	=(U11+M12)*EXP((B12*0.075+(1-B12)*0.03)*(30/	=(Y11)*EXP(Y4*(30/360	=(Z11+C12+D12-G12-H12-I12-J12-K12-L12-M12-N12-O12-P12)*EXP(
13	=(Q12-I13)*EXP(Q4*(30/36	=(U12+M13)*EXP((B13*0.075+(1-B13)*0.03)*(30/	=(Y12)*EXP(Y4*(30/360	=(Z12+C13+D13-G13-H13-I13-J13-K13-L13-M13-N13-O13-P13)*EXP(
14	=(Q13-I14)*EXP(Q4*(30/36	=(U13+M14)*EXP((B14*0.075+(1-B14)*0.03)*(30/	=(Y13)*EXP(Y4*(30/360	=(Z13+C14+D14-G14-H14-I14-J14-K14-L14-M14-N14-O14-P14)*EXP(
15	=(Q14-I15)*EXP(Q4*(30/36	=(U14+M15)*EXP((B15*0.075+(1-B15)*0.03)*(30/	=(Y14)*EXP(Y4*(30/360	=(Z14+C15+D15-G15-H15-I15-J15-K15-L15-M15-N15-O15-P15)*EXP(
16	=(Q15-I16)*EXP(Q4*(30/36	=(U15+M16)*EXP((B16*0.075+(1-B16)*0.03)*(30/	=(Y15)*EXP(Y4*(30/360	=(Z15+C16+D16-G16-H16-I16-J16-K16-L16-M16-N16-O16-P16)*EXP(

You should repeat this process for each column, which should represent each individual credit card, student loan, auto loan, and home loan, and all Roth IRAs, 401ks, taxable investments, HSAs, and checking accounts. Keep in mind that the underlying formulas for liability accounts, asset accounts, and cash accounts before accounting for interest are all different as we already reviewed.

Updating Your Cash Flow Projections

Congratulations! Now you have your financial projections established, you can foresee your financial situation into the future, and you are able to make a financial plan for your goals. Just after each month, you should review your projections you had for the previous month and overwrite it with actualities. If your income, expenses, or account transfers were different than you had projected, you should overwrite it. If your account balances were different than you had projected, you should overwrite the formula with the actual balance the account had at the very end of the month. If you notice your actualities are different than your projections for several months in a row—which is common for expenses—it may be time to update your budgets (such as your budgeted expenses in Mint.com or whatever online aggregated personal finance manager you use). This exercise will likely take you less than 10 minutes each month and is the only continual work you'll need to ensure your financial plan is on track to reach your goals.

Financial Priorities

1. Automate expense tracking and establish categorized budgets to control and predict your spending.
2. **Project your finances to reveal the future impact of your spending and saving.**

Chapter 4 – Bank Account Buffer and Checking Accounts

Bank Account Buffer

The very first place to save money is in the place it's most liquid—a checking account. Your first savings priority is to save one month's income in a checking account. Often called a "bank account buffer," these savings prevent you from living paycheck-to-paycheck and enable you to automate your account transfers through monthly autopay without risk of overdraft fees.

Assuming your monthly account transfers are no more than one month's income (you can't spend or save cash you don't have), having one month's income available ensures your checking account balance will never fall below $0 in any month even if all your monthly account transfers happen at the beginning of the month before that month's first paycheck. Even if you overspend your budget shortly before the end of the month, if you are paid biweekly you will not be at risk of depleting your checking account. If you are paid less frequently, you'll want to ensure your bank account buffer includes one additional paycheck such as two months' income for a monthly paycheck. You can avoid depleting your bank account buffer by ensuring your financial projections never allow your checking account to fall below your bank account buffer by the end of each month; otherwise, you need to lower the cash you are applying elsewhere such as to expenses or paying down debt.

Checking Accounts

The most important aspect of a good checking account is easy access to your cash. The institution you bank with for your checking account should have a plethora of ATMs located all over where you can withdraw cash without fees. In 2015, Money Magazine named Aspiration.com's Summit

Account the best checking account available.[7] The Summit Account will allow you to use any ATM in the world for free since Aspiration reimburses all ATM fees. The account also offers very high yearly interest rates for checking accounts: 1% for entire balances that're over $2,500 and 0.25% for entire balances that're under that. Aspiration also donates 10% of their profits to charity.

If your bank account buffer is under $2,500, you might want to consider Bank5Connect.com's checking account that reimburses ATM fees up to $15 per month and offers 1% interest rates for entire balances that're over $100. While a few other banks and credit unions offer higher checking account interest rates, they usually only do so after requiring a number of debit card purchases each month and as you'll see in Chapter 7 – Credit Cards, we'll prefer to use credit cards for our purchases to earn rewards.

Financial Priorities

1. Automate expense tracking and establish categorized budgets to control and predict your spending.
2. Project your finances to reveal the future impact of your spending and saving.
3. **Save one month's income in an easily accessible checking account as a bank account buffer.**

[7] http://time.com/money/collection-post/4079857/best-checking-bank-account-aspiration-2015/

Chapter 5 – 401(k)s

Understanding Income and Capital Gains Taxes

While taxes are necessary for running a civilized society, they are likely your largest expense. For every dollar of income you earn, 10-37% of it never makes it into your checking account. Below is a table of income tax brackets by tax filing status and income for 2018.

Marginal Tax Rate	Single	Married Filing Jointly	Head of Household*	Married Filing Separately
10%	$0-$9,525	$0-$19,050	$0-$13,600	$0-$9,525
12%	$9,525-$38,700	$19,050-$77,400	$13,600-$51,800	$9,525-$38,700
22%	$38,700-$82,500	$77,400-$165,000	$51,800-$82,500	$38,700-$82,500
24%	$82,500-$157,500	$165,000-$315,000	$82,500-$157,500	$82,500-$157,500
32%	$157,500-$200,000	$315,000-$400,000	$157,500-$200,000	$157,500-$200,000
35%	$200,000-$500,000	$400,000-$600,000	$200,000-$500,000	$200,000-$300,000
37%	Over $500,000	Over $600,000	Over $500,000	Over $300,000

Note: To qualify as "Head of Household", you must have all the following apply: a) Pay for more than half of the household expenses, b) Be considered unmarried for the tax year, c) You must have a qualifying child or dependent.[8]

Your "marginal tax rate" is what people refer to when they say what "tax bracket" you are in. It's the highest percentage of your income you pay

[8] https://turbotax.intuit.com/tax-tools/tax-tips/General-Tax-Tips/Guide-to-Filing-Taxes-as-Head-of-Household/INF23153.html

towards income taxes, but not all your income is taxed at this high percentage. If you are single, your first $9,525 is taxed at a 10% rate, your next $9,525 to $38,700 is taxed at a 12% rate, and this pattern continues up until those earning $500,000 or more have that amount of their income taxed at a 37% rate. Your "effective tax rate" is the taxes you pay divided by your gross income and it'll be lower than your marginal tax rate. When you deduct from your taxable income, for example by making contributions to a 401(k), you are reducing your taxable income starting from the last dollar you earned and therefore are avoiding paying the larger marginal tax rate.

But income tax isn't the only tax you pay when you accumulate wealth. Any realized gains on investments—that is, money earned from selling an investment for more money than you bought it—is also taxed. This is called "capital gains tax." Your capital gains tax rate depends on your income. Add your capital gains to your income to find your long-term capital gains tax rate.

Long-Term Capital Gains Rate	Single Taxpayers	Married Filing Jointly	Head of Household	Married Filing Separately
0%	Up to $38,600	Up to $77,200	Up to $51,700	Up to $38,600
15%	$38,600-$425,800	$77,200-$479,000	$51,700-$452,400	$38,600-$239,500
20%	Over $425,800	Over $479,000	Over $452,400	Over $239,500

Note: An additional 3.8% net investment income tax (NIIT) may apply if you meet one of the following: a) You file a joint tax return or use the qualifying widow(er) status with more than $250,000 in modified adjusted gross income (MAGI), b) You are married filing separately with more than $125,000 in MAGI, or c) You are single or head-of-household with more than $200,000 in MAGI.[9]

Similar to the progressive income tax bracket system, your capital gains will be taxed starting at your capital gains tax rate and will continue at that rate

[9]https://www.fool.com/taxes/2017/12/22/your-guide-to-capital-gains-taxes-in-2018.aspx

until your capital gains bump you up into a tax bracket associated with a higher capital gains tax rate. As you can see, long-term capital gains tax rates are lower than income tax rates, but in order for a capital gain to qualify for the preferable long-term capital gains tax rate, you must have owned the investment for at least a year before selling it; otherwise, your gains are considered short-term capital gains and are subject to your higher income tax rate instead. Furthermore, any interest or dividends gained from checking/savings accounts or non-municipal bonds are considered income and taxed as income. To incentivize investing in stocks, the government classifies dividends from stocks from U.S. companies with normal company structures (corporations) and some foreign corporations that benefit from U.S. tax treaties as "qualified dividends" that are only subject to the lower long-term capital gains tax rates.[10]

Luckily, there are vehicles that allow you to protect your income and capital gains from taxes and these vehicles are the best way of increasing your net worth without decreasing your expenses or increasing your income.

Defined Contribution Plans: 401(k)s, 403(b)s, 457s, and TSPs

401(k)s

Many employers offer 401(k) investment accounts through a third party financial institution called an "administrator" as a tax-deferred investment vehicle to encourage you to save for retirement. The money you contribute is removed from your paycheck *before* taxes are applied to your paycheck and therefore the money isn't taxed before being invested. Money you withdraw from your 401(k) is considered income and is taxed as income at that moment, which is why 401(k)s are called "tax-deferred" accounts. Whether you opt to route some money from your paycheck to a 401(k) or route that money to your checking account then a taxable investment account, you will pay income taxes on that money eventually. Moreover, whether you pay income tax at time of paycheck or at time of 401(k) withdrawal doesn't change the net amount you earn (assuming the same tax rate at time of paycheck and withdrawal) after withdrawing the money.

[10] http://www.dividend.com/dividend-education/qualified-vs-unqualified-dividends/

So how do you save on taxes? The realized gains on taxable investments are subject to capital gains taxes whereas the realized gains on 401(k) investments are not. You save by not having to pay capital gains taxes of 15-20% on your investment gains, depending on your tax bracket. This 15-20% savings can have a significant impact—much greater than 20%—on the net amount you earn thanks to the power of compound interest. Your investment accounts earn a percentage of your account balance. Those earnings also grow your account balance and so you earn even more money on those earnings. This has an exponential effect that over long periods of time can make you very wealthy. While the same exponential effect happens with taxable accounts, any realized capital gains are taxed 15-20% every year, creating a "tax drag" on your otherwise faster exponential growth with tax-advantaged accounts such as 401(k)s.

Below is a hypothetical example from Goldman Sachs comparing the balance of a $200,000 tax-advantaged account to a $200,000 taxable account over 25 years.[11]

Over 25 years, the tax-advantaged account has $349,000 or over 51% more in it than the taxable account! Even after only 5 years, the tax-advantaged

---

[11] https://www.gsam.com/content/gsam/us/en/advlsors/market-lnslghts/gsam-connect/2016/the-power-of-tax-deferral-why-it-may-pay-to-delay.html

account has $22,000 or over 8% more in it than the taxable account. The difference between the accounts is the 20% long term capital gains tax dragging down the returns of the taxable account. This example's assumptions exaggerate the balance differences when compared to the average investor, but the underlying impact of tax drag on a compounding balance remains the same nonetheless.

To ensure 401(k)s aren't overly abused, the government caps how much money you can contribute to a 401(k) each year. In 2018, the limit is $18,500 per year but the limit changes each year. Furthermore, a catch-up contribution is allowed for those age 50 or older to contribute more in their later years as they come closer to reaching retirement. In 2018, that catch-up contribution is an additional $6,000 per year on top of the original $18,500 per year.[12] Your employer is responsible for ensuring your contributions don't exceed the yearly limit and so you may see less of your paycheck contributed to your 401(k) towards the end of the year if you've already reached the yearly cap.

Withdrawal

So what's the catch? The government allows employers to offer the 401(k) vehicle to encourage employees to save for retirement. To protect from employees abusing this vehicle for purposes other than retirement, the government charges a penalty of 10% (in addition to taxing your withdrawal as income) on any amounts you withdraw from a 401(k) account prior to age 59 ½. This makes 401(k) accounts bad for investing any money you'll need within around the next 10 years (before age 59 ½) because the additional earnings of no tax drag are likely to be outweighed by the penalty. But what if you'd like to retire before age 59 ½? ½? The government provides a means of withdrawing your 401(k) early without penalty by rolling it over to a Roth IRA which we'll discuss in Chapter 8 – Emergency Funds, Shor-Term Goals, IRAs, and Taxable Accounts.[13]

---

[12] https://www.irs.gov/newsroom/irs-announces-2018-pension-plan-limitations-401k-contribution-limit-increases-to-18500-for-2018

[13] https://www.irs.gov/retirement-plans/plan-participant-employee/retirement-topics-tax-on-early-distributions

Some 401(k) administrators allow you to borrow from your 401(k) without paying taxes or penalties, but you would need to pay the amount back with interest, usually within five years. Furthermore, some administers won't allow you to make 401(k) contributions until the loan is repaid which would cause you to miss out on any employer matches and tax deferrals from those missed contributions. If you quit or are terminated from your employer, you must repay your 401(k) loan within 60 days or your loan will be considered a withdrawal subject to taxes and penalties.[14] Because of these negatives, loans from 401(k)s are rarely a good idea.

403(b)s, 457s, and TSPs

Whereas 401(k)s are defined contribution plans offered by corporations, 403(b)s are offered by nonprofit organizations, 457s for state and municipal employees, and Thrift Savings Plans (TSPs) for federal employees. All the plans are very similar and can be interchanged when I mention 401(k) throughout this book, but there are some minor differences. 403(b)s allow an additional catch up contribution of $3,000 per year for up to five years after working in the same nonprofit for at least fifteen years and if the employee contributed less than $5,000 on average per year previously. 457s have no early withdrawal penalty and some state and municipal workers have access to a 457 *and* a 401(k) or 403(b) and can contribute up to $18,500 *each* into both plans. Thrift Savings Plans (TSPs) are just like 401(k)s and the funds offered in TSPs are very low fee.[15]

Roth 401(k)s

In addition to tax-deferred or "Traditional" 401(k)s some employers offer tax-exempt or "Roth" 401(k)s. The money you contribute to a Roth 401(k) is removed from your paycheck *after* taxes are applied to your paycheck and therefore the money is taxed before being invested. Money you withdraw from your Roth 401(k) isn't considered income and is never taxed again, which is why Roth 401(k)s are called "tax-exempt" accounts. The yearly cap for 401(k)s applies across both Traditional and Roth 401(k)s such that you

[14] http://www.myretirementpaycheck.org/Navigating-Retirement-Crises/What-You-Need-to-Know-Before-Borrowing-From-Your

[15] http://money.cnn.com/retirement/guide/401kandCos/?iid=EL

can contribute a maximum of $18,500 a year (plus an additional $6,000 if you're 50 or older) total across both kinds of accounts.

If you contribute an amount to a Traditional 401(k) or that same amount but removing taxes from it before putting it into a Roth 401(k), the two accounts would earn you the same amount of money after withdrawing from them assuming you are in the same tax bracket at time of withdrawal as you were at time of contribution. Because Traditional 401(k)s are taxed at time of withdrawal and Roth 401(k)s are taxed at time of contribution, the decision of whether to contribute to a Traditional vs Roth 401(k) comes down to predicting if your taxes will be higher or lower in retirement.

Choosing Traditional vs Roth 401(k)

Many financial advisors recommend younger individuals in lower tax brackets choose a Roth 401(k) over a Traditional 401(k) because incomes typically grow over time and you may end up withdrawing more money at a higher tax bracket in retirement than your earnings today. These same advisors often point to how taxes in 2018 are historically lower than in the past and they believe taxes will need to go up over time, so you might as well pay them while they're low. Furthermore, if you have the means to contribute more than the $18,500 limit to a Traditional 401(k), you might want to opt for a Roth 401(k) because the limit applies after taxes have been taken out, effectively allowing you to save more in a Roth 401(k) than in a Traditional 401(k).

All of that is sound advice; however, there is a scenario where I'd strongly recommend contributing to a Traditional 401(k) over a Roth 401(k). If you plan on retiring early, you will need to live well below your means so that you can contribute a large percentage of your income to savings. This means the expenses necessary to maintain your standard of living in retirement will be well below your current yearly income and you won't need to withdraw much from your 401(k) each year in retirement. Therefore, it's likely you will fall into a lower tax bracket in retirement because your income—your Traditional 401(k)withdrawals—will be lower than your current income, making it advantageous to contribute to a Traditional 401(k) to avoid paying high taxes now in favor of paying low taxes in retirement. If taxes do not increase in the future, many people can avoid paying a 22% or more income tax now in favor of paying a 15% or less income tax in retirement. For those looking to retire early, this possibility alone trumps the arguments for a Roth 401(k).

Employer Matching

You setup contributions to a 401(k) through your employer and they will remove the funds you specify, either a percentage of your paycheck or a set dollar amount, from your paycheck and put them into your 401(k) account. Many employers offer a 401(k) match which is by far the best "optional" deal you will come across. I put optional in quotes because you should not consider it optional after you've built a bank account buffer: no exceptions. Employers who match typically offer a 100% match-rate matching dollar for dollar the amount you contribute to your 401(k) up to a certain percentage of your salary which is often between 3-6%. That is an immediate 100% return on your investment. The match is free money for you since your employer contributes money into your 401(k) that you otherwise would not have gotten if you didn't contribute. Note that when your company matches your Roth 401(k) contributions, their match will go into your Traditional 401(k) since matches are not allowed to go into your Roth 401(k).

Although in general funding a 401(k) should be done after you've saved up an emergency fund and have paid down your credit card debt, the exception is contributing up to the maximum employer match because the immediate 100% return (or 50% return for some employers) beats out any interest rate a credit card would charge you. Yes, I'd rather see you max out your employer match into a 401(k) account and stay in credit card debt longer than get out of credit card debt early and miss out on the match's free money.

Choosing 401(k) Investments

There's a big secret in the investment world: investment fund managers can't beat the market after their fees. Warren Buffett has been making this point since 2007 when he challenged Protégé Partners, an asset management firm, to a bet of $500,000 for charity. Buffet would invest in a low-fee passively managed index fund designed to track the market (S&P

500). Protégé Partners would invest in an actively managed fund of hedge funds with high fees. After ten years, whatever fund had the highest returns, wins. At the end of 2017 when the bet concluded, Buffett won with returns of 99% over Protégé Partners' paltry 24%.[16]

The same pattern applies to almost all actively managed funds. In 2018 the S&P Dow Jones Indices ran a study of domestic stock funds to compare their performance after fees against market benchmarks. It found that over a one-year period, 63.46% of large-cap managers, 54.18% of mid-cap managers, and 72.88% of small-cap managers underperformed the S&P 500, the S&P MidCap 400, and the S&P SmallCap 600, respectively. So on average, actively managed funds underperformed the market over the short term, but what about the long term? Actively managed funds perform even worse over the long term. Over a five-year period, 76.49% of large-cap managers, 81.74% of mid-cap managers, and 92.90% of small-cap managers lagged their respective benchmarks. Over a fifteen-year period, 92.43% of large-cap managers, 95.13% of mid-cap managers, and 97.70% of small-cap managers lagged their respective benchmarks.[17]

Could it be that a top minority of smart active managers are consistently beating the market such that you only need to identify a consistently winning fund to ensure you'll beat the market? The S&P Dow Jones Indices also runs a study called "The Persistence Scorecard" to see if winning funds can consistently outperform their benchmarks to differentiate luck from skill. Out of funds that were in the top quartile after a 12-month period two years prior only 2.33% managed to stay in the top quartile both of the following two 12-month periods when randomly we would have expected 6.25%. Even out of the top half of funds only 16.25% managed to stay in the top half both of the following two 12-month periods when randomly we would have expected 25%. Fund performance is also inconsistent over longer periods. Out of funds that were in the top quartile after a 12-month period four years prior only 0.18% managed to stay in the top quartile through all four of the following 12-month periods when randomly we would have expected 0.39%. Maybe outperforming the benchmark in *every*

[16] https://www.fool.com/investing/2018/01/03/warren-buffett-just-officially-won-his-million-dol.aspx
[17] https://us.spindices.com/documents/spiva/spiva-us-mid-year-2018.pdf

12-month period is asking too much and instead we just want our fund to remain in the top quartile or at least the top half of funds after our five-year period. Unfortunately, the results still show a lower consistency than luck. Out of funds that were in the top quartile after a 5-year period 5 years prior only 18.96% remained in the top quartile when randomly we would have expected 25%. Out of funds that were in the top half after a 5-year period 5 years prior only 42.45% remained in the top half when randomly we would have expected 50%.[18]

Known as the "SPIVA Scorecard," the S&P Dow Jones Indices releases the same studies every year and year after year it shows that active managers don't beat the market after their fees over long periods and if they do they can't do it consistently, making the case their outperformance was due to luck. Therefore, investors are better off investing in funds that track the market for as low of fees as possible. Such funds are called "index funds." A large number of investors resist investing in index funds because money is very personal and they believe they should strive to be "better than average." As Burton Malkiel, a famous economist and writer, puts it "It's true that when you buy an index fund, you give up the chance to boast at the golf course that you picked the best performing stock or mutual fund. That's why some critics claim that indexing relegates your results to mediocrity. In fact, you are virtually guaranteed to do better than average." He further explains, "Why does indexing outmaneuver the best minds on Wall Street? Paradoxically, its because the best and brightest in the financial community have made the stock market very efficient. When information arises about individual stocks or the market as a whole, it gets reflected in stock prices without delay, making one stock as reasonably priced as another."[19]

Fees

If fund managers can't beat the market after their fees, how do they make money? Fees! This means your goal in selecting assets for your 401(k) should be to mimic the market with as low of fees as possible. Even a 1% fee can drag down your compounding considerably in the long run. A $100,000

[18]https://us.spindices.com/documents/spiva/persistence-scorecard-march-2018.pdf
[19]https://www.aei.org/publication/more-evidence-that-its-really-hard-to-beat-the-market-over-time-95-of-finance-professionals-cant-do-it/

balance with over 30 years compounded annually in a fund charging 1% fees would yield over $135,000 less than it would in a fund charging 0.25% fees.[20]

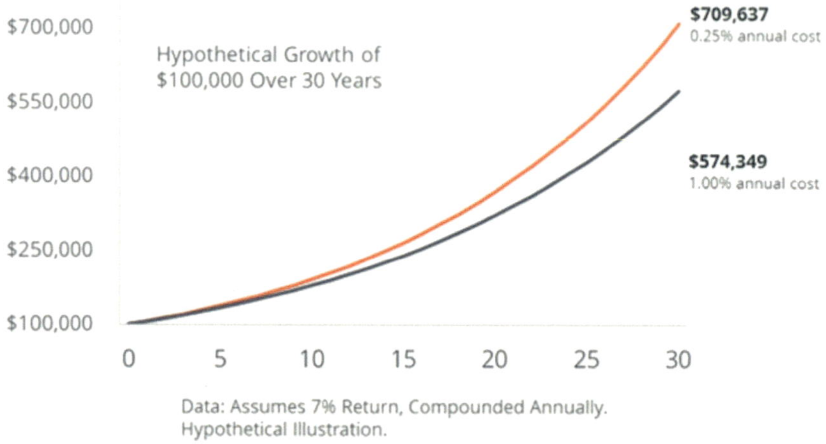

Controlling Volatility

In addition to high fees, volatility can also wreak havoc on your medium-term investment returns. The table below shows 5 examples in order of increasing volatility of the impact of dispersed returns on a $10,000 balance. The simple average return for each example is 10% but the compound average return is lower the higher the volatility.[21]

[20] http://www.sefgroup.com/Retirement-Plans.2.htm

[21] http://www.investopedia.com/articles/06/compoundingdarkside.asp

Impact Of Dispersion

Start With $10,000	Example 1		Example 2		Example 3		Example 4		Example 5	
	Return	Total Value	Return	Total Value	Return	Total Value	Return	Total Value	Return	Total Value
Year 1	10%	$11,000	10%	$11,000	5%	$10,500	30%	$13,000	40%	$14,000
Year 2	10%	$12,000	20%	$13,200	25%	$13,125	-20%	$10,400	30%	$18,200
Year 3	10%	$13,310	0%	$13,200	0%	$13,125	20%	$12,480	-40%	$10,920
Simple Average Return		10%		10%		10%		10%		10%
Compound Average Return		10.00%		9.70%		9.49%		7.66%		2.98%

The lower compound average return associated with higher volatility is caused by one of two reasons: experiencing your high returns too early when your portfolio is small for less compound interest or experiencing your losses too late when your portfolio is large for more compound loss. For these reasons, you want to try to reduce volatility by diversifying your investments. For example, investing in both domestic stocks and international stocks is likely to yield an overall steadier portfolio than a portfolio built entirely from either asset class alone since these two asset classes' values sometimes diverge trajectories with one upwards and one downwards due to market forces. Even though both asset classes can expect roughly the same return, the combined portfolio experiences less volatility.

This is the primary conjecture of Modern Portfolio Theory, which assumes the market is efficient (we already showed it is too efficient for active managers to beat) and states that a rational investor who cared about minimizing volatility while maximizing returns should own the so-called "global market portfolio" and its relative proportions of domestic and international stocks.[22] US stocks make up about 42% of the global stock market capitalization.[23] To match the global stock market portfolio you should allocate 42% of your stock exposure to domestic stocks and 58% to international stocks.

Because stocks are a high-volatility asset class, the percentage of your net worth you should allocate to stocks depends on your appetite for risk. The more willing you are to allow your net worth to fall, the more you should

---

[22] http://blog.alphaarchitect.com/2017/06/14/passive-investing-theory-practice-global-market/#gs.SbyvNR8

[23] http://wdi.worldbank.org/table/5.4

allocate towards stocks in return for their higher expected yield. Your appetite for risk is probably driven by how far you are from retirement. Most people eventually set a target retirement date. Target retirement dates bode for increased risk when younger that over time should achieve high returns and decreased risk when older so you're confident a market crash won't severely delay your target retirement date by costing you a significant portion of your now large nest-egg like we saw in Example 5 in the table above.

The highest yielding low-volatility alternative to stocks is bonds, making them a good asset class to compare stocks against. Bonds are loans made to governments or corporations in exchange for the promise of repayment with interest. Bonds are highly unlikely to outperform stocks over longer than a 30-year period as stocks beat bonds in 99.3% of all 30-year periods and even 95.8% of all 20-year periods from 1871 to 2012 as shown in the figure below.[24]

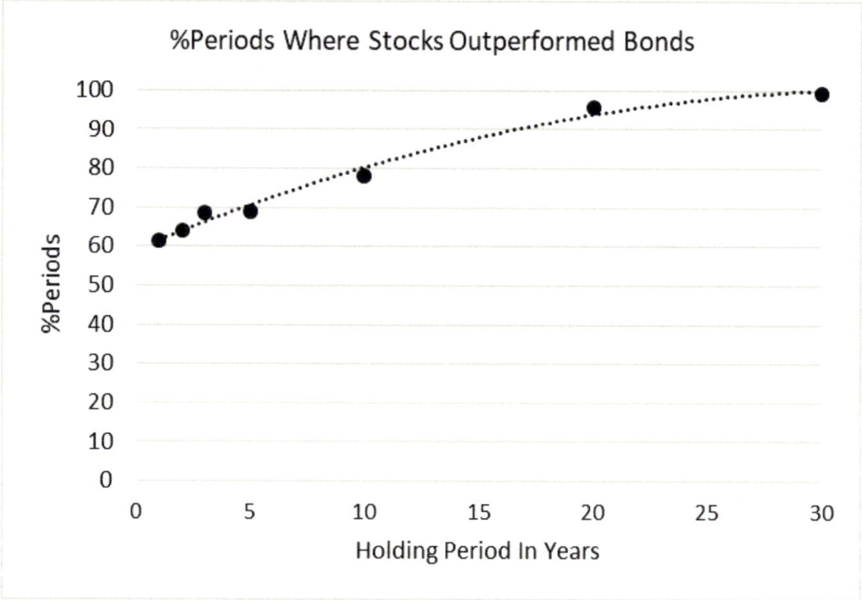

[24] https://www.vox.com/personal-finance/2014/7/22/5877329/less-than-a-quarter-of-americans-get-the-most-important-investment

If you are more than 30 years from retirement, you should invest 100% in stocks with no bonds. Once you anticipate (possibly from your financial projections) that you are within 30 years from retirement, it is best to use a decelerating "glide path" that decreases stock allocation each year until retirement. The shorter your time to retirement, the greater the risk that your stocks won't outperform your bonds by your target retirement date, putting your retirement date at risk. This risk also rises at a faster rate the closer you get to retirement, making it prudent to lower your stock allocation faster as you approach retirement. For example, decreasing your stock allocation by 1% a year until you're 10 years from retirement, then by 2% a year until reaching a 60% stock allocation upon retirement is a good strategy that helps mitigate retirement date risk. Even if you already have a portfolio and you haven't done this stock decrease, you should estimate how far you are from retirement and set your equity exposure accordingly based upon the figure below to ensure you can safely retire around your target date.

Besides mitigating retirement date risk, targeting a low stock allocation when starting retirement also mitigates sequence of return risk. Sequence of return risk is the risk that shortly after retirement—when your portfolio is largest—a market crash could cause any further investment gains in retirement to be minimal due to your diminished portfolio size. Allocating more of your investments to bonds around your target retirement date protects you from any bear market that could delay your retirement or diminish the longevity of your nest-egg. These risk periods can be seen over a typical portfolio's lifetime in the figure below.[25]

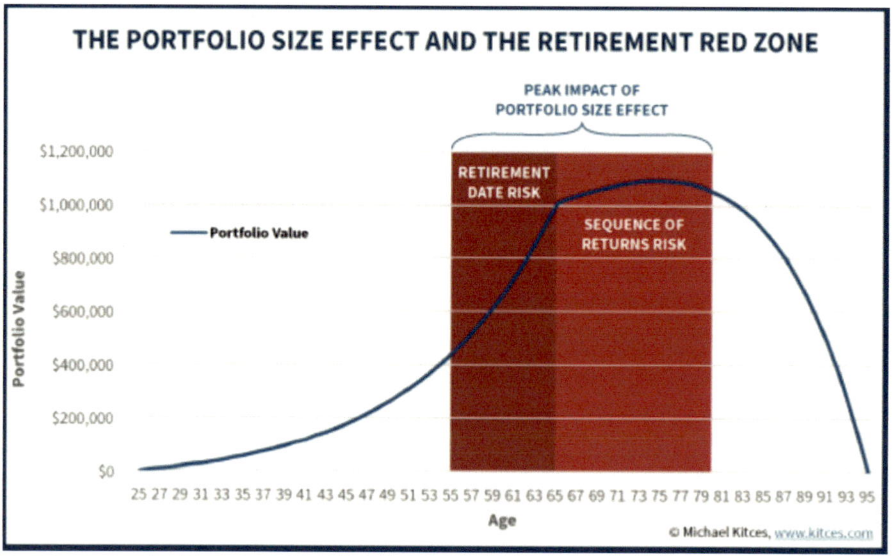

The percentage of stocks to hold at retirement and how to adjust your allocation during retirement are topics that have recently garnered scrutiny. The commonly accepted approach is to maintain your allocation throughout retirement or possibly even continue to decrease stock allocation as you age. More recently, studies have found that slowly increasing stock allocation after retirement as you age through and past the sequence of

[25]https://www.kitces.com/blog/managing-portfolio-size-effect-with-bond-tent-in-retirement-red-zone/

returns risk window gives portfolios the additional gains needed to increase the longevity of your portfolio.

Karsten Jaske, a financial advisor and blogger at EarlyRetirementNow.com, laid out what such "rising equity glidepaths" look like for 30-yearretirements. In particular he assessed glidepaths starting at 20%, 40%, 60%, or 80% stocks rising to 80% or 100% stocks over a few different rate increases including 0.2%, 0.3%, 0.4%, and 0.5% increases per month. Because rising equity glidepaths protect against overvalued markets in early retirement, he compared markets with Cyclically Adjusted Price-to-Earnings (CAPE) ratios above 20—highly valued markets—to those below 20—lowly valued markets. Although it has its flaws, the CAPE ratio (for which Robert Shiller won the Nobel Prize in Economics in 2013)[26] is the price of stocks divided by their average earnings over the last 10 years and is arguably the best estimator for market valuations. To ensure the glidepaths completely ride out high stock valuations, he also compared active stock increases, limiting increases to when the S&P500 index is below its all-time high, against passive stock increases, increasing regardless of stock valuations. He examined safe withdrawal rates for a 25%, 10%, 5%, and 1% failure rate as well as a fail-safe option with no chance of failure. Which failure rate you choose is up to your comfort, but most research falls into the 5% failure rate because the majority of the time your portfolio grows much larger than you need and in the minority of the times it does not, it's due to falling victim to sequence of returns risk after the first decade and you can make small adjustments to spending to right the ship thereafter.

[26] https://www.nobelprize.org/nobel_prizes/economic-sciences/laureates/2013/press.html

	SWR Percentiles conditional on CAPE>20					SWR Percentiles conditional on CAPE<=20				
	Min (fail-safe)	1%	5%	10%	25%	Min (fail-safe)	1%	5%	10%	25%
60% fixed	3.78%	3.84%	3.95%	4.01%	4.38%	3.83%	3.98%	4.39%	4.62%	5.24%
65% fixed	3.83%	3.86%	3.97%	4.06%	4.43%	3.87%	4.05%	4.44%	4.71%	5.37%
70% fixed	3.83%	3.88%	3.98%	4.08%	4.50%	3.91%	4.08%	4.47%	4.77%	5.49%
75% fixed	3.82%	3.88%	3.98%	4.10%	4.45%	3.95%	4.13%	4.50%	4.82%	5.62%
80% fixed	3.65%	3.87%	3.98%	4.10%	4.42%	3.99%	4.18%	4.53%	4.86%	5.71%
85% fixed	3.45%	3.82%	3.98%	4.08%	4.43%	4.02%	4.22%	4.55%	4.90%	5.82%
90% fixed	3.25%	3.72%	3.93%	4.03%	4.38%	4.05%	4.24%	4.57%	4.95%	5.94%
95% fixed	3.05%	3.55%	3.88%	3.99%	4.37%	4.07%	4.27%	4.58%	4.97%	6.06%
100% fixed	2.85%	3.35%	3.81%	3.95%	4.32%	4.10%	4.27%	4.59%	4.98%	6.15%
60->80%, 0.2%, pass.	3.85%	3.89%	4.01%	4.13%	4.57%	3.99%	4.15%	4.53%	4.79%	5.62%
60->80%, 0.3%, pass.	3.86%	3.90%	4.00%	4.10%	4.59%	4.01%	4.17%	4.55%	4.82%	5.67%
60->80%, 0.2%, actv.	3.89%	3.93%	4.03%	4.16%	4.58%	3.99%	4.15%	4.54%	4.78%	5.57%
60->80%, 0.3%, actv.	3.86%	3.90%	4.02%	4.13%	4.58%	4.01%	4.17%	4.56%	4.82%	5.62%
80->100%, 0.2%, pass.	3.66%	3.87%	4.01%	4.10%	4.51%	4.11%	4.28%	4.63%	4.97%	6.02%
80->100%, 0.3%, pass.	3.63%	3.87%	3.98%	4.10%	4.53%	4.13%	4.30%	4.64%	4.99%	6.07%
80->100%, 0.2%, actv.	3.66%	3.91%	4.04%	4.14%	4.53%	4.11%	4.28%	4.63%	4.95%	5.96%
80->100%, 0.3%, actv.	3.63%	3.88%	4.01%	4.10%	4.52%	4.13%	4.30%	4.66%	4.98%	6.03%
40->80%, 0.3%, pass.	3.89%	3.90%	4.00%	4.12%	4.40%	3.89%	4.05%	4.43%	4.67%	5.30%
40->80%, 0.4%, pass.	3.84%	3.86%	3.98%	4.10%	4.47%	3.92%	4.08%	4.46%	4.73%	5.42%
40->80%, 0.3%, actv.	3.90%	3.95%	4.04%	4.11%	4.37%	3.89%	4.04%	4.42%	4.63%	5.16%
40->80%, 0.4%, actv.	3.91%	3.93%	4.02%	4.13%	4.44%	3.93%	4.09%	4.46%	4.69%	5.24%
60->100%, 0.3%, pass.	3.91%	3.95%	4.08%	4.20%	4.65%	4.07%	4.23%	4.61%	4.87%	5.85%
60->100%, 0.4%, pass.	3.86%	3.90%	4.02%	4.16%	4.63%	4.12%	4.27%	4.63%	4.92%	5.95%
60->100%, 0.3%, actv.	3.96%	4.00%	4.11%	4.23%	4.69%	4.08%	4.23%	4.62%	4.84%	5.73%
60->100%, 0.4%, actv.	3.94%	3.98%	4.10%	4.23%	4.62%	4.12%	4.27%	4.64%	4.90%	5.83%
20->80%, 0.4%, pass.	3.79%	3.87%	3.92%	4.00%	4.27%	3.77%	3.92%	4.22%	4.46%	4.96%
20->80%, 0.5%, pass.	3.83%	3.85%	3.91%	4.01%	4.35%	3.83%	3.98%	4.25%	4.55%	5.08%
20->80%, 0.4%, actv.	3.75%	3.86%	3.92%	3.99%	4.22%	3.75%	3.89%	4.18%	4.35%	4.80%
20->80%, 0.5%, actv.	3.83%	3.91%	3.96%	4.02%	4.28%	3.81%	3.95%	4.22%	4.41%	4.90%
40->100%, 0.4%, pass.	3.95%	3.96%	4.06%	4.21%	4.55%	3.98%	4.14%	4.51%	4.75%	5.44%
40->100%, 0.5%, pass.	3.90%	3.92%	4.02%	4.17%	4.65%	4.04%	4.20%	4.55%	4.82%	5.56%
40->100%, 0.4%, actv.	3.97%	3.99%	4.09%	4.20%	4.50%	3.97%	4.13%	4.48%	4.70%	5.24%
40->100%, 0.5%, actv.	3.99%	4.00%	4.10%	4.24%	4.57%	4.02%	4.18%	4.54%	4.75%	5.34%
30->70%, 0.11%, pass.	3.56%	3.68%	3.79%	3.88%	4.10%	3.60%	3.73%	4.10%	4.28%	4.65%
30->70%, 0.2%, pass.	3.68%	3.81%	3.89%	3.97%	4.20%	3.72%	3.86%	4.22%	4.40%	4.87%
30->70%, 0.3%, pass.	3.77%	3.85%	3.92%	4.00%	4.27%	3.77%	3.92%	4.27%	4.52%	5.04%
30->70%, 0.4%, pass.	3.81%	3.82%	3.91%	4.03%	4.30%	3.80%	3.95%	4.31%	4.58%	5.15%
20->60%, 0.11%, pass.	3.40%	3.51%	3.67%	3.74%	3.96%	3.46%	3.59%	3.89%	4.04%	4.36%
20->60%, 0.2%, pass.	3.53%	3.65%	3.78%	3.85%	4.06%	3.59%	3.73%	4.02%	4.19%	4.60%
20->60%, 0.3%, pass.	3.62%	3.73%	3.81%	3.90%	4.12%	3.65%	3.79%	4.10%	4.30%	4.79%
20->60%, 0.4%, pass.	3.71%	3.76%	3.83%	3.90%	4.14%	3.68%	3.82%	4.13%	4.37%	4.91%

The results show that for the worst retirement scenario (CAPE > 20 and a potential market crash looming), portfolios with a 60% stock allocation that increases around 0.3% per month until reaching a 100% stock allocation after 12 years had the highest safe withdrawal rate, starting around 4.11% then increased over time with inflation.[27]

Even for longer retirement periods, the same rising equity glidepath remains the winner, just with a smaller safe withdrawal rate starting around 3.63% then increased over time with inflation. Below is the same analysis done for 60-year retirements.

[27] https://earlyretirementnow.com/2017/09/20/the-ultimate-guide-to-safe-withdrawal-rates-part-20-more-thoughts-on-equity-glidepaths/

	SWR Percentiles conditional on CAPE>20					SWR Percentiles conditional on CAPE<=20				
	Min (fail-safe)	1%	5%	10%	25%	Min (fail-safe)	1%	5%	10%	25%
60% fixed	3.03%	3.21%	3.32%	3.41%	3.61%	3.15%	3.27%	3.66%	3.86%	4.18%
65% fixed	3.11%	3.30%	3.37%	3.45%	3.66%	3.21%	3.35%	3.75%	3.96%	4.33%
70% fixed	3.19%	3.35%	3.42%	3.48%	3.69%	3.27%	3.42%	3.80%	4.04%	4.47%
75% fixed	3.25%	3.36%	3.45%	3.51%	3.72%	3.32%	3.49%	3.87%	4.13%	4.58%
80% fixed	3.14%	3.36%	3.47%	3.53%	3.71%	3.37%	3.54%	3.91%	4.20%	4.70%
85% fixed	3.02%	3.31%	3.47%	3.53%	3.74%	3.41%	3.59%	3.95%	4.27%	4.82%
90% fixed	2.88%	3.24%	3.43%	3.51%	3.76%	3.44%	3.64%	3.97%	4.31%	4.93%
95% fixed	2.74%	3.14%	3.37%	3.48%	3.79%	3.47%	3.67%	4.00%	4.35%	5.03%
100% fixed	2.58%	3.03%	3.29%	3.45%	3.80%	3.49%	3.69%	4.01%	4.37%	5.10%
60->80%, 0.2%, pass.	3.30%	3.40%	3.50%	3.55%	3.81%	3.36%	3.49%	3.90%	4.14%	4.62%
60->80%, 0.3%, pass.	3.32%	3.41%	3.50%	3.55%	3.84%	3.38%	3.52%	3.91%	4.16%	4.65%
60->80%, 0.2%, actv.	3.28%	3.43%	3.50%	3.57%	3.81%	3.37%	3.50%	3.91%	4.12%	4.58%
60->80%, 0.3%, actv.	3.34%	3.41%	3.51%	3.56%	3.83%	3.38%	3.51%	3.93%	4.15%	4.64%
80->100%, 0.2%, pass.	3.32%	3.45%	3.54%	3.61%	3.85%	3.50%	3.67%	4.04%	4.35%	5.05%
80->100%, 0.3%, pass.	3.29%	3.44%	3.53%	3.59%	3.85%	3.52%	3.69%	4.05%	4.36%	5.04%
80->100%, 0.2%, actv.	3.32%	3.47%	3.57%	3.64%	3.87%	3.50%	3.68%	4.06%	4.35%	5.02%
80->100%, 0.3%, actv.	3.29%	3.45%	3.54%	3.62%	3.86%	3.52%	3.69%	4.06%	4.37%	5.06%
40->80%, 0.3%, pass.	3.19%	3.33%	3.43%	3.52%	3.75%	3.27%	3.40%	3.77%	3.97%	4.43%
40->80%, 0.4%, pass.	3.27%	3.37%	3.43%	3.51%	3.77%	3.29%	3.43%	3.79%	4.04%	4.52%
40->80%, 0.3%, actv.	3.18%	3.32%	3.45%	3.53%	3.73%	3.27%	3.39%	3.75%	3.92%	4.31%
40->80%, 0.4%, actv.	3.23%	3.37%	3.45%	3.55%	3.76%	3.31%	3.44%	3.78%	3.98%	4.42%
60->100%, 0.3%, pass.	3.44%	3.50%	3.61%	3.67%	3.95%	3.47%	3.61%	4.01%	4.26%	4.90%
60->100%, 0.4%, pass.	3.42%	3.46%	3.57%	3.69%	3.93%	3.50%	3.63%	4.03%	4.31%	4.97%
60->100%, 0.3%, actv.	3.42%	3.54%	3.63%	3.67%	3.97%	3.47%	3.61%	4.01%	4.23%	4.82%
60->100%, 0.4%, actv.	3.47%	3.52%	3.63%	3.69%	3.96%	3.51%	3.65%	4.04%	4.28%	4.90%
20->80%, 0.4%, pass.	3.08%	3.19%	3.38%	3.43%	3.71%	3.17%	3.29%	3.56%	3.74%	4.19%
20->80%, 0.5%, pass.	3.16%	3.27%	3.36%	3.42%	3.73%	3.22%	3.34%	3.61%	3.80%	4.32%
20->80%, 0.4%, actv.	3.05%	3.15%	3.29%	3.40%	3.56%	3.15%	3.27%	3.50%	3.63%	3.98%
20->80%, 0.5%, actv.	3.11%	3.22%	3.32%	3.43%	3.60%	3.20%	3.33%	3.56%	3.69%	4.14%
40->100%, 0.4%, pass.	3.33%	3.47%	3.54%	3.63%	3.87%	3.38%	3.51%	3.87%	4.12%	4.66%
40->100%, 0.5%, pass.	3.41%	3.47%	3.53%	3.62%	3.90%	3.43%	3.56%	3.91%	4.18%	4.77%
40->100%, 0.4%, actv.	3.30%	3.43%	3.54%	3.65%	3.85%	3.36%	3.49%	3.85%	4.05%	4.49%
40->100%, 0.5%, actv.	3.36%	3.50%	3.58%	3.67%	3.89%	3.41%	3.54%	3.89%	4.10%	4.58%
30->70%, 0.11%, pass.	2.83%	2.95%	3.09%	3.27%	3.48%	2.96%	3.07%	3.34%	3.48%	3.77%
30->70%, 0.2%, pass.	2.97%	3.10%	3.25%	3.38%	3.59%	3.09%	3.20%	3.52%	3.67%	4.01%
30->70%, 0.3%, pass.	3.05%	3.18%	3.34%	3.40%	3.64%	3.14%	3.26%	3.58%	3.75%	4.18%
30->70%, 0.4%, pass.	3.13%	3.24%	3.33%	3.41%	3.62%	3.16%	3.28%	3.61%	3.81%	4.28%
20->60%, 0.11%, pass.	2.67%	2.76%	2.89%	3.08%	3.34%	2.80%	2.87%	2.98%	3.13%	3.44%
20->60%, 0.2%, pass.	2.81%	2.92%	3.04%	3.25%	3.50%	2.94%	3.05%	3.26%	3.41%	3.67%
20->60%, 0.3%, pass.	2.89%	2.99%	3.15%	3.28%	3.56%	2.99%	3.11%	3.36%	3.54%	3.88%
20->60%, 0.4%, pass.	2.97%	3.07%	3.22%	3.27%	3.54%	3.01%	3.13%	3.40%	3.58%	4.00%

In general, the practice supports having lower stock exposure when your balance is highest to protect your nest-egg from volatility-caused retirement date risk and sequence of return risk then growing stock exposure as your balance shrinks over retirement to give it the extra yield needed for greater longevity. For now, what is important is that you should adjust your stock allocation to suit your risk based on your estimated years to retirement and slowly lower your stock allocation to a target of 60% stocks at retirement to mitigate retirement date risk and sequence of return risk.

Investing in Bonds

A bond is a loan to a government or corporation in exchange for their promise to pay periodic interest payments until repayment of the loan upon the bond's maturity date. Not all bonds are created equal. Bonds are subject to a set of risks for which investors demand higher returns for taking on. The most fundamental of these risks is "credit risk" or the likelihood that the government or corporation will repay your loan. Bonds issued by the U.S. Treasury are backed by the full faith and credit of the U.S. government and therefore considered to have no credit risk. Furthermore, unlike high-yield corporate bonds which tend to correlate with stocks because both are impacted by the performance of corporations (corporations doing well are more likely to repay the loan)[28], U.S. Treasury bonds tend to negatively correlate with stocks[29] making them ideal for softening the volatility of stocks and providing you more assets during stock market downswings to sell and buy the now cheap stocks.[30]

U.S. Treasury bonds come in three major asset classes: short-term (bonds maturing in less than 3 years), intermediate-term (bonds maturing in 3-10 years), and long-term (bonds maturing in 10-30 years). The longer the bond term, the greater the "interest rate risk," which is the risk that the Fed will increase interest rates making any newly issued bonds promising higher periodic interest payments more attractive to investors and any already

---

[28] http://www.etf.com/sections/index-investor-corner/swedroe-truth-about-credit-premiums
[29] https://www.marketwatch.com/story/why-many-bond-funds-are-as-volatile-as-stocks-2014-12-06
[30] https://www.kitces.com/blog/stress-testing-a-diversified-portfolio-to-properly-evaluate-risk-exposure/

existing bonds less attractive and worth less if sold prior to maturity. If interest rates rise, investors already in short-term bonds have few low-interest payments remaining before their loan is repaid and they can soon use that repayment to buy the more attractive bonds; whereas investors already in long-term bonds will have many low-interest payments remaining before they can do the same. To compensate investors for taking on interest rate risk, long-term bonds come with higher interest payments.[31]

The problem is that long-term bonds' interest rate risk subject them to greater volatility, which is exactly what you were looking to avoid by investing in bonds in the first place. Michael Kitces, financial planner at Pinnacle Advisory Group and blogger at Kitces.com, showed that during times of falling interest rates equity/bond portfolios with long-term treasury bonds had the highest safe withdrawal rate in retirement and during times of rising interest rates equity/bond portfolios with short-term treasury bonds had the highest safe withdrawal rate in retirement. Since future interest rates are not very predictable, Kitces favors avoiding long-term bonds because in the worst-case (lowest safe withdrawal rate) scenario, short-term treasury bonds (called Treasury Bills) had a higher safe withdrawal rate than long-term treasury bonds (called Treasury Bonds).

---

[31] https://www.forbes.com/sites/rickferri/2014/07/02/the-risk-of-short-term-bond-funds

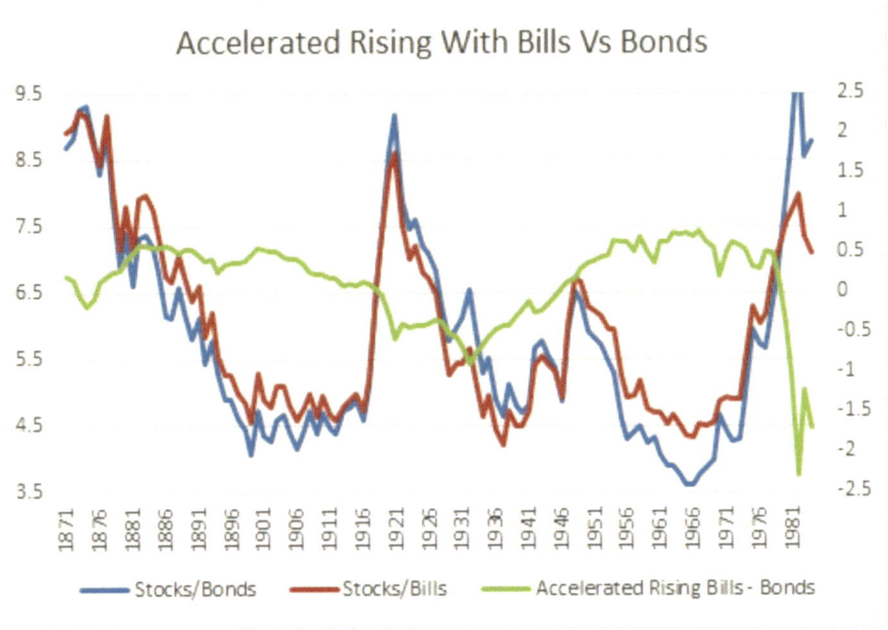

Part of the problem with long-term treasury bonds is that interest rates taper off as maturity lengths increase, making a curve known as the "yield curve." That is, as you take on more and more interest risk, you get less and less interest yield in return.[32]

[32] https://www.forbes.com/sites/wadepfau/2017/01/31/what-is-the-bond-yield-curve/#4b74022a55f9

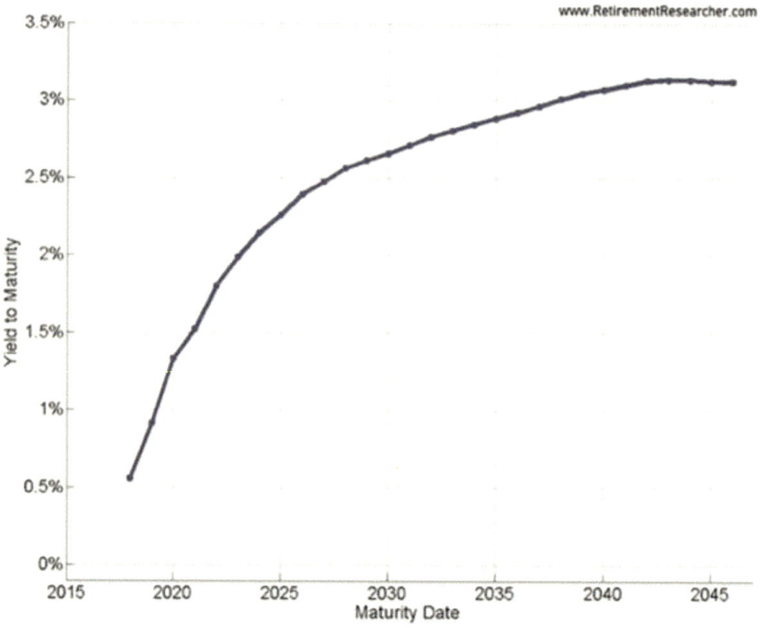

As you can see, the yield curve is almost a straight line for the first 5 years, tapers off in years 6-10, and begins to flatten out years 11-30. This yield curve makes bonds that mature right around the 5-year mark, typically held by intermediate term funds, the sweet spot of getting the most yield for the least risk according to notable financial theorist William Bernstein.[33]

Unlike stocks, treasury bonds do not benefit from diversification. Whereas stocks (and corporate bonds for that matter) comprise of unsystematic risk, which is risk that can be diversified away, treasury bonds mostly comprise of systematic risk, which cannot be diversified away. Larry Swedroe, in his book "The Only Winning Bond Strategy You'll Ever Need," demonstrates the concept using a farmer and his crops. A farmer cannot diversify away the risk that flood, drought, insects, plague, or other adverse effect destroys his crops (systematic risk), but he can diversify away the risk that his returns are diminished (unsystematic risk) due to falling soybean prices by also planting

---

[33] http://www.mypersonalfinancejourney.com/should-use-short-term-or-intermediate-term-bonds-fixed-income-allocation/

corn, wheat, and sorghum. Since treasuries comprise of systematic risk that cannot be diversified away, we'll likely do best to exclusively pick the treasury term most suited to act as ballast to our stocks, which is whatever term provides the best combination of the least correlation with stocks and the least volatility. Over the 35 years prior to 2015, intermediate treasuries have tended to provide the best combination of being negatively correlated with stocks (-1 correlation is best) and low-volatility (0 beta is best) as shown in the graphic below, making intermediate treasury bonds the bond class of choice.[34]

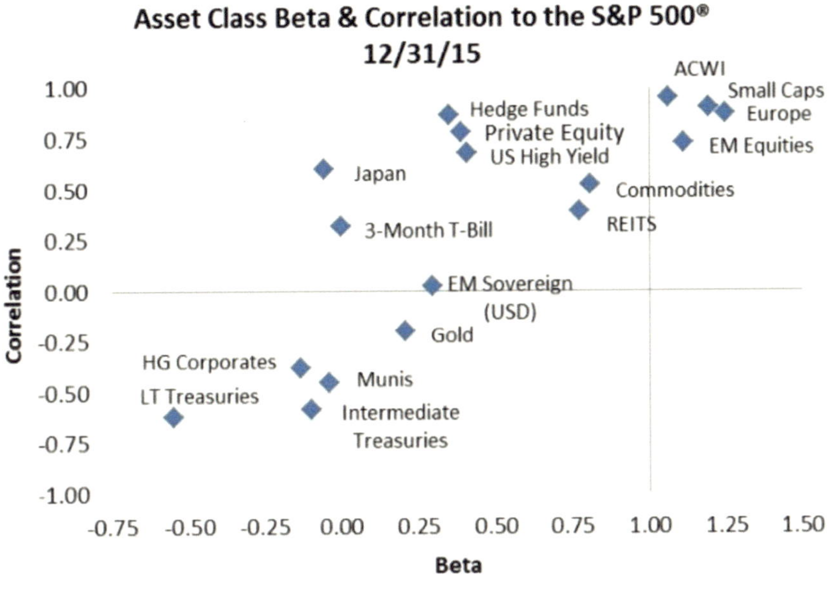

In 1997 the U.S. Treasury started offering Treasury Inflation Protected Securities (TIPS). TIPS are treasury bonds that hedge against inflation based on the Consumer Price Index such that when inflation is higher than expected the value of TIPS goes up and when inflation is lower than

[34] http://www.fortunefinancialadvisors.com/blog/long-term-bonds-behave-more-like-stocks-than-you-might-think

expected the value of TIPS goes down. This makes TIPS safer over the long run than the "nominal" bonds discussed previously. However, when the market crashes it also experiences deflation which is bad for TIPS. This makes TIPS not as good as nominal bonds for diversifying against stocks.[35]

If your 401(k) doesn't offer an intermediate-term treasury nominal bond fund with an expense ratio that is at least within 0.1% of the cheapest bond fund offered, you should favor the cheaper bond fund. Usually the lowest fee bond fund will reflect domestic bonds. If you do venture into international bond funds you need to make sure they are currency hedged, which means they are immune to currency volatility; otherwise, the currency volatility can erase the portfolio steadiness you are trying to gain with bonds.[36] Currency hedging tends to make international bond funds more expensive than domestic bond funds, rendering international bond funds unnecessary for your portfolio.

Market Efficiency Factor Anomalies

The truth is, the market has not historically been perfectly efficient. Back testing over many decades has shown that a handful of stock "factors" have tended to yield slightly higher risk-adjusted returns than the market portfolio[37]:

1. Value
    a. Inexpensive stocks outperform expensive stocks.
2. Low volatility
    a. Less volatile stocks outperform the most highly volatile stocks.
3. Momentum
    a. Winning stocks keep winning; losing stocks keep losing.
4. Illiquidity
    a. Stocks with higher trading costs outperform stocks with lower trading costs.

---

[35] https://obliviousinvestor.com/tips-vs-nominal-treasury-bonds/

[36] https://www.betterment.com/resources/investment-strategy/why-international-bonds-but-not-currency-risk-belong-in-your-portfolio/

[37] https://www.researchaffiliates.com/en_us/publications/articles/223_finding_smart_beta_in_the_factor_zoo.html

The reason these factors have yielded higher returns comes down to two highly debated reasons: additional risk and/or mispricing.[38] Value and momentum factors have beaten the market with higher volatility favoring the argument that at least some of their additional yield can be attributed to a premium reward rational investors demand for taking on increased risk. Likewise, investors might demand a premium for taking on the risk of decreased liquidity. Since these premiums had come with a disproportionately low amount of risk, it can be argued that you can achieve a higher return for the same amount of risk as the global market portfolio by increasing the weight of these factors in the equity portion of your portfolio to increase returns and increase the bond percentage of your portfolio to maintain the portfolio's risk.

However, if the premium is caused by mispricing, which must be the case for the low volatility factor, then as investors recognize and exploit these anomalous factors the premium becomes diminished. The problem with factor investing is that unlike the market portfolio, it is not macro-consistent: that is, it cannot be held by all investors without disturbing market prices. Factor investing has become more popular in recent years with marketers even coining terms such as "value tilt" or "smart beta" to help sell it. The increased popularity and resulting increased price of each factor can negate or even inverse its historical premium in the future. This seems likely to have already happened with these factors.

The illiquidity factor is theorized to have been arbitraged away by high frequency trading.[39] The momentum factor premium was calculated without considering the high trading costs associated with its necessary turnover which tends to overcome its premium.[40] The low-volatility factor stocks now come with higher costs than in the past, causing many to feel that while they still predict low-volatility, they likely no longer produce a

[38]https://money.usnews.com/money/blogs/the-smarter-mutual-fund-investor/articles/2017-04-06/key-considerations-of-smart-beta-investing

[39]http://www.etf.com/sections/index-investor-corner/swedroe-liquidity-premium-diminishing?nopaging=1

[40]https://www.researchaffiliates.com/en_us/publications/journal-papers/312_will_your_factor_deliver_an_examination_of_factor_robustness_and_implementation_costs_factor_zoology.html

premium.[41] This leaves the value factor. Its premium is certainly up for debate. Many advisors believe the value premium is caused by investors' infatuation with and overpricing of glamour growth stocks and that this infatuation will persist into the future. I believe this was the case in the past and that the value premium, like has been shown with all the other more than 500 factor premiums—including the size factor premium[42]—assessed by academics, has been diminishing and will eventually be negated as value tilting gains popularity and accessibility and the market becomes more efficient. Regardless, factor tilting takes on a *known* increase of risk and fees in exchange for the *belief* that a factor premium will persist into the future. This added risk can be mitigated by taking on a lower stock allocation in your portfolio, but again you're trading a *known* premium (equity market exposure) for a *believed* premium.

Rick Ferri, a renowned advisor and advocate of value tilting, advises those who factor tilt to allocate no more than 25% of their stock allocation towards factor tilts away from the global market portfolio. He believes such a value tilt might produce a 0.25% yearly premium on average and it might take up to 30 years to see the premium.[43] This means if the funds available in your 401(k) to overweight value stocks come with fees of 0.25% greater than the global market funds, it's not advisable to value tilt at all regardless of whether you believe the value premium will persist into the future.[44] In summary, if you do factor tilt do so lightly, but I'd advise not factor tilting at all and instead opting to industry tilt.

Total Economy Portfolio

Similar to factor tilts are industry tilts, the most popular of which is the Real Estate Investment Trust (REIT) tilt. While reflected in total market portfolios, Real Estate represents about 13% of the U.S. economy with only about 4% traded on public markets. Therefore, to reflect the total economy, it's advisable to have a REIT index fund represent about 9% of your stock allocation to make up the difference not captured in your total market

---

[41] http://www.etf.com/sections/index-investor-corner/swedroe-use-caution-low-vol-strategies?nopaging=1
[42] https://www.researchaffiliates.com/en_us/publications/articles/284_busting_the_myth_about_size.html
[43] http://time.com/money/3859334/value-investing-tilt/
[44] https://www.bogleheads.org/forum/viewtopic.php?t=143109

funds. Additionally, venture capital investments represent about 3% of the U.S. economy and are not traded on public markets. The best proxy for venture capital is small-cap value index funds. Therefore, it's advisable to have a separate small-cap value index fund represent about 3% of your stock allocation. The reason the total market portfolio in theory gave the best return for the least risk was because it diversified your investments in proportion to the wisdom (investments) of the crowd. With these industry tilts, your portfolio will more closely represent the broader crowd wisdom (total economy) instead of just the investments made available to the public market.

Portfolio Management

After you figure out your appropriate stock exposure and desired asset allocation among that stock exposure, you need to translate this into a dollar amount for each asset class in your portfolio. The percentage of your net worth to keep in stocks isn't the same as the percentage of your investment portfolio to keep in stocks. Your net worth includes other assets such as your house and car and liabilities such as your credit cards, student loans, and mortgage. To this point we've been discussing how much of your net worth to keep in stocks, but to manage your investment portfolio of stocks and bonds you'll need to translate this to a percentage of your portfolio to keep in stocks. You can calculate this like so:

[Target percent of portfolio in stocks] = ([Target percent of net worth in stocks] * [Net worth]) / [Total portfolio value]

If you have a positive net worth outside of your 401(k), your 401(k) stock allocation will be higher than your portfolio allocation and if you have a negative net worth outside of your 401(k), your 401(k) stock allocation will be lower than your portfolio allocation. If your net worth *including* your 401(k) is negative, you should assume 100% of your portfolio should be in stocks while you build up a positive net worth.

To determine your portfolio's REIT, small-cap value, domestic, and international stock percentages after accounting for bond allocation, multiply your stock split percentage, whether REIT, small-cap value, domestic, or international, by your portfolio stock allocation. For example, if you are 20 years from retirement with a $0 net worth outside your investment portfolio, you are targeting 90% stocks and of your 90% stocks you are targeting 9% REITs, 3% small-cap value, 37% (42% * (100%-12% tilted)) domestic and 51% (58% * (100% - 12% tilted)) international. Therefore, you should find the lowest fee fund offered by your 401(k) that tracks the REIT market and allocate 8.1% (9% * 90%) of your portfolio to it, the lowest fee fund that tracks small-cap value stocks and allocate 2.7% (3% * 90%) of your portfolio to it, the lowest fee fund that tracks the U.S. market and allocate 33.3% (37% * 90%) of your portfolio to it, and the lowest fee fund that tracks the international market and allocate 45.9% (51% * 90%) of your portfolio to it, and either an intermediate-term treasury bond fund or the lowest fee bond fund and allocate 10% of your portfolio to it.

As your investments experience gains or losses, your portfolio's allocation percentages will deviate from your target. Therefore, you should rebalance your portfolio at least yearly.[45] Oftentimes your 401(k) administrator will provide an "automatic rebalancing" service that you can sign up for that will rebalance your portfolio to your target percentages on a regular basis. If it doesn't offer automatic rebalancing, check in yearly and ensure you sell your funds above your percentage allocation to buy those below your percentage allocation.

The goal of rebalancing is to adjust your exposure to risk. Since stocks usually see the most growth, rebalancing most often involves selling stocks to buy bonds, decreasing your volatility. When stocks crash, rebalancing involves selling bonds to buy the now cheaper stocks, increasing your expected returns. On average, rebalancing causes you to sell more stocks and buy more bonds, effectively lowering your expected returns but also your volatility, which is why you should rebalance.[46]

It has been argued that rebalancing among asset classes with similar returns, such as between domestic and international stocks, increases returns because of "regression to the mean" a phenomenon where volatile, uncorrelated assets tend to trend towards their expected return and so realizing gains from your "winning stocks" and investing those gains into your now cheaper "losing stocks" can earn you more than the combined

---

[45] http://www.vanguard.com/pdf/icrpr.pdf

[46] https://www.kitces.com/blog/how-rebalancing-usually-reduces-long-term-returns-but-is-good-risk-management-anyway/

expected return of those assets.[47] This concept is controversial and the little evidence supporting it shows only a small increase in gains; however, rebalancing for volatility control is a well-supported concept.[48]

Financial Priorities

1. Automate expense tracking and establish categorized budgets to control and predict your spending
2. Project your finances to reveal the future impact of your spending and saving.
3. Save one month's income in an easily accessible checking account as a bank account buffer.
4. **If your employer matches contributions to your 401(k), contribute up to the maximum match for free money and invest it in low fee global market stock portfolio and domestic bond funds, increasing bond allocation as you approach retirement.**

---

[47] http://www.efficientfrontier.com/ef/996/rebal.htm

[48] https://www.advisorperspectives.com/newsletters14/pdfs/Does_Rebalancing_Really_Pay_Off.pdf

Chapter 6 – Credit

After taking advantage of any free money your employer offers as a 401k match, most will have some kind of debt to pay down. Many advisors refer to debt as bad or even evil; I consider it a tool. Debt is a means to leverage money when you have little of it, to invest in yourself and your family. When used to invest in assets such as businesses or rental properties it can provide a positive return. Similarly, when used to invest in personal assets such as necessary food, clothing, shelter, transportation, and education, it can provide a return not only in happiness but also in getting and keeping a job. The drawback being that debt comes with interest charges, which like stocks and bonds compounds, but negatively to your net worth. How "bad" the debt is depends on how much you let that debt compound. Compounding depends on size, rate, and duration. To control the size of your debt, you must set and follow budgets as mentioned in Chapter 2 – Budgeting. To control the rate, you must maintain a good credit score, which is the focus of this chapter. To control the duration, you must pay debt down as we'll cover in Chapter 7 – Credit Cards and Chapter 12 – Paying Down "Good" Debt.

Your credit score provides lenders a means to measure how risky you are to lend to. Scores range from 300 to 850 and the higher your credit score the less risky you are to lenders for making payments on time and not defaulting on your debt. Your credit score impacts whether or not banks will offer you good credit cards. It also impacts your interest rate when you take out any loan such as a mortgage for a home. If you have a credit score of 650 and get a 30-year, $400,000 mortgage, you could pay over $70,000 more in interest than someone with a 750 credit score and the same mortgage.[49] The most popular credit scoring system is known as the FICO score because it was developed by the Fair Isaac Corporation.[50] Lenders report your credit card, loan, and mortgage information to credit agencies such as Equifax, Experian, and TransUnion and they use this information to

[49] https://www.creditkarma.com/article/why-your-credit-score-matters
[50] http://www.finra.org/investors/how-your-credit-score-impacts-your-financial-future

calculate your credit score. A credit score of 800 – 850 is considered excellent, 740 – 799 is very good, 670 – 739 is good, 580 – 669 is fair, and 579 and below is poor.[51]

Finding Your Credit Score

To increase your credit score you first should find what your credit score is. The best credit reporting sites are ones like CreditKarma.com that let you check your score as often as you'd like for free. Credit Karma provides you your credit score from TransUnion and Equifax and also offers you insight into your behaviors that are impacting your credit score. They offer this for free to build an audience and they make money by providing lenders a platform to advertise loan offers to that audience. First, ensure your loan history is accurate. A survey by the U.S. Public Interest Research Group found that 25% of reports have serious errors, 30% listed old accounts that should have been deleted, and 79% had some sort of mistake or error.[52] If you find an error, contact the respective credit bureau, whether TransUnion or Equifax, and challenge the error. Once your history is accurate, you will want to take steps to increase your score.

Increasing Your Credit Score

Payment History

Timely payments are the biggest factor that goes into calculating your credit score as they make up 35% of your FICO score.[53] According to FICO data, a 30-day delinquency could cause as much as a 90- to 110-point drop on a FICO Score of 780 for a consumer who has never missed a payment on any credit account.[54] Each payment that is more than 30 days late can be reported to a credit reporting agency. At the very least, to maintain your financial health you absolutely must pay the minimum monthly payment on each of your credit cards. Ensuring this happens is very easy when you setup

---

[51] http://www.experian.com/blogs/ask-experian/infographic-what-are-the-different-scoring-ranges/
[52] https://www.amazon.com/dp/B000PC71Q4
[53] http://www.creditcards.com/credit-card-news/fico-credit-score-payment-history-1270.php
[54] http://blog.equifax.com/credit/can-one-late-payment-affect-my-credit-score/

automatic payments from your checking account for your credit cards and loans through their respective bank websites. You should ensure you have automatic payments setup not only for the credit cards you regularly use, but also the cards you do not use to ensure you're safe in case any unexpected charges come up on those unused credit cards.

Credit Card Utilization

Next to avoiding late payments, the biggest factor that goes into calculating your credit score is your credit card utilization ratio, or the percentage of your available credit card credit limit that's used up as outstanding balances. It makes up 30% of your FICO score.[55] You should aim to have less than 30%–and ideally less than 10%–of your available credit card credit limit in outstanding balances.

One approach to reducing your credit card utilization ratio is to pay down your outstanding balances, which we'll cover in Chapter 7 – Credit Cards. The other approach is to increase your available credit. Increasing your available credit can be as simple as calling your credit card company and asking them to increase your credit limit for cards you already have. Because individual card utilization is also taken into account, start with the card with the highest utilization and work your way down to the card with the least until your credit card utilization is under 30%. Be aware that as you apply for more credit from more banks, the amount of credit and likelihood of increasing your limit goes down, but at least you're improving your credit card utilization ratio regardless of whether you can get it below 30% by asking for credit limit increases.

An alternative is to apply for more credit through a new credit card. Applying for more credit can temporarily decrease your credit score a little bit because it often indicates to lenders that an applicant needs more credit to cover their expenses because their expenses are greater than their income. Because you built a budget and forecasted your future finances, we know this is not the case for you and as you do not increase your credit card balance for about six months your credit score will recover and surpass

---

[55] http://www.creditcards.com/credit-card-news/credit-utilization-fico-1270.php

what it would have become had you maintained a utilization ratio above 30%.

Length of Credit History

The length of your credit history accounts for 15% of your FICO score. To lenders, the longer the history of your credit, the more information and confidence they have in your payment history. The minimum amount of credit history needed to generate a FICO score is one account for six months.[56] An account must be on your credit report in order to affect your FICO score. Closed accounts that were always paid on time remain on credit reports for ten years from the date of closure or last account update, while accounts with late payments remain for seven years from the date of first delinquency.[57] This means you should never close your accounts even if they are for credit you never use because their history (and credit limit) improves your credit score. This also means you should open a credit account even if you don't need the credit because it will start generating credit history for you. A perfect account would be a rewards credit card, which we'll discuss in Chapter 7 – Credit Cards.

Amount of New Credit

New credit you've acquired in the past 6 - 12 months makes up 10% of your FICO score. It incorporates the following[58]:

- How many accounts have been opened in the past 6 - 12 months, as well as the proportion of accounts that are new, by account type.
- How long it's been since the opening of any new accounts, by account type.
- How many credit inquiries have been made recently.
- How long it's been since any credit inquiries.
- The re-appearance on a credit report of positive credit information for an account that had earlier payment problems.

[56] http://www.creditcards.com/credit-card-news/length-credit-history-fico-score.php
[57] http://www.creditcards.com/credit-card-news/length-credit-history-fico-score.php
[58] http://www.creditcards.com/credit-card-news/fico-score-new-credit-loan-inquiry-1270.php

We already reviewed how opening accounts can temporarily hurt your credit score but the long-term benefits—assuming the new credit is handled responsibly—outweigh the temporary hit your credit score takes. I also don't want you to worry about credit inquiries. Credit inquiries happen when you explore taking on additional credit and the lender looks up your credit score and its details to ensure you qualify for the additional credit they're offering you. This is known as a "hard credit inquiry." "Soft credit inquiries" are inquiries that are not intended for checking if you qualify for credit–such as when a bank pulls your credit to verify your identity or when you check your credit score on Credit Karma—and do not impact your credit score. Most hard credit inquiries result in a credit score decrease of fewer than 5 points. Also, multiple hard credit inquiries made within 45 days are treated as a consumer comparison shopping for credit offers and after 30 days these are all treated as a single hard inquiry on your credit score. Shopping around for good credit offers far outweighs the impact it has on your credit score and you should instead focus on improving your other credit score factors.

Credit Mix

Lastly, your credit mix makes up the remaining 10% of your FICO score. Lenders overall feel that if you have a good credit history with a variety of loan account types, you are less risky to lend to. These account types include auto loans, student loans, furniture loans, mortgage loans, bank credit cards, retail credit cards, gas station credit cards, and rental data (note that debit cards don't build up credit history with a credit bureau). It's not worth taking on a loan with a balance to just to increase your credit mix, but applying for a new account type with no balance such as a retail credit card you intend to pay in full every month can provide a small boost to your credit score.

Financial Priorities

1. Automate expense tracking and establish categorized budgets to control and predict your spending.
2. Project your finances to reveal the future impact of your spending and saving.

3. Save one month's income in an easily accessible checking account as a bank account buffer.
4. If your employer matches contributions to your 401(k), contribute up to the maximum match for free money and invest it in low fee global market stock portfolio and domestic bond funds, increasing bond allocation as you approach retirement.
5. **Monitor and increase your credit score.**

Chapter 7 – Credit Cards

Now that you've taken advantage of the easy ways to increase your credit score, it's time to pay down your high interest debt. Credit cards usually have yearly interest rates between 12% and 25% depending on your credit score and no other investment we'll discuss after this point is likely to net you more than a 12% return. Luckily, if you've been able to keep your credit score up, you have options to avoid paying these high interest rates while you pay down your balance.

Avoiding Interest While Paying Down Credit Card Debt

Many credit cards offer introductory interest rates of 0% for up to 12-21 months. The harder part about these cards is getting the balance off your interest cards and onto these no interest cards. Most of these cards have a balance transfer fee of 2-5% the transfer amount. While paying 2-5% upfront is favorable to paying 12% over the course of a year, there are ways to avoid these fees. The easiest way is to get a credit card that has no balance transfer fee like the Chase Slate card[59] that also offers a 0% interest rate for 18 months.[60] Be sure if you find a similar card that it offers 0% interest on both purchases *and* balance transfers. However, if such a card is not an option, any 0% interest rate card will work if you use it for purchases and use your income to pay down your interest cards, effectively avoiding any direct balance transfer from happening.

You should rotate through these 0% interest rate cards until you are free of credit card debt.[61] If you time this right (which you can do using your financial projections we created in Chapter 3 – Projecting Finances) you can avoid paying credit card interest while paying down credit card debt for over a decade. Pay down your highest interest rate cards first. Some advisors argue that you should pay down your lowest balances first. They

---

[59] https://creditcards.chase.com/credit-cards/chase-slate

[60] https://wallethub.com/credit-cards/no-balance-transfer-fee/

[61] https://www.creditkarma.com/creditcards/explore?categoryID=1&pgsz=0&pubKey=RFSVDJ8NOUC11YT1&adposition=1t2

are appealing to the psychological wins of paying off an entire credit card balance. If you feel quickly paying down more cards will encourage you to save more money for paying down credit card debt, by all means do that; however, if you have a set amount you can use to pay down debt, it's beneficial to pay down your highest interest rate card first as that card's interest is compounding faster and is costing you the most money. Be sure to setup every card on autopay set to the minimum payment for all cards except the card you're trying to pay down. Allocate the maximum acceptable monthly amount to that card based upon your financial projections after maintaining a bank account buffer and contributing up to your maximum employer 401(k) match.

Another means of lowering interest rates is to call your credit card company and ask for a lower rate. If you've been increasing your credit score, they may just offer you a lower rate. If a card has an annual or monthly fee, you often can get that fee removed just by asking. The exception might be if the card offers a lot of rewards, since that fee might be what keeps the credit card company from losing an unacceptable amount of money to you.

Rewards Credit Cards

Once you have paid off your credit card debt, you should still use credit cards for expenses and pay off their balance monthly. In particular, you want to use rewards credit cards. The best are usually cashback rewards credit cards but if you travel frequently you might want to consider a travel rewards credit card. The offers on these cards will change over time but you can refer to NerdWallet.com as a reputable source for up to date rewards offerings.[62]

Overall Purchases

The best cashback rewards credit cards today offer 2% cashback on all purchases. This is like a permanent 2% coupon on *everything* you charge to the card and it adds up.

---

[62] https://www.nerdwallet.com/blog/top-credit-cards/nerdwallets-best-rewards-credit-cards/

Discover It®

The Discover it® card[63] is the best cash rewards card I've found for the first year. It offers 5% cash back on quarterly rotating categories and 1% cash back on all other purchases. Where this card really shines is that they *double* your cash back rewards for the first year of use for 10% cash back on quarterly rotating categories and 2% back on everything else.

Citi® Double Cash Visa or Fidelity® Rewards Visa Signature®

The Citi® Double Cash card[64] pays you 1% cash rewards as you spend and another 1% cash rewards as you pay off the balance for an effective 2% cash back rate. The Fidelity® Rewards Visa Signature® card[65] offers 2% cash rewards as you spend, but you need to redeem the rewards into a fidelity account (bank account or investment account). You can transfer from the Fidelity bank account into another bank account right away, but the extra hassle makes me slightly favor the Citi® Double Cash Visa card.

Chase Freedom®

The Chase Freedom® visa card[66] pays you 5% cash back on quarterly rotating categories and 1% cash back on all other purchases. In itself this offer is not all that great compared to other cash back rewards cards, but when paired with the Chase Sapphire Preferred® travel rewards card the offer is better. You can transfer points among cards and the Chase Sapphire Preferred® provides you a 25% bonus when you spend points for booking airfare, hotels, rental cars, or cruises. This means your 5% cash back on rotating categories turns into 6.25% cash back.

Groceries, Gas, and Dining

Blue Cash Preferred from American Express

The Blue Cash Preferred® card[67] from American Express offers 6% cash rewards on groceries, 3% at U.S. gas stations, then 1% on all other purchases. This card does come with a $95 yearly fee, but groceries and gas

---

[63] https://www.discover.com/credit-cards/cash-back/it-card.html
[64] https://www.citi.com/credit-cards/credit-card-details/citi.action?ID=citi-double-cash-credit-card
[65] https://www.fidelity.com/go/rewards-visa-signature
[66] https://creditcards.chase.com/credit-cards/chase-freedom
[67] https://card.americanexpress.com/bcp/

usually make up enough of most people's spending to make this card worth it. It also comes with a 0% interest rate for 12 months on purchases and 0% on balance transfers, but it does charge a 3% balance transfer fee.

Capital One Savor℠

The Capital One Savor℠ card[68] offers 4% cash rewards on dining and entertainment, 2% on groceries, then 1% on all other purchases. It also comes without a yearly fee, making it a great card for those who often dine out.

Travel

Chase Sapphire Preferred®

The Chase Sapphire Preferred® Visa card[69] offers 2 "miles" per dollar on travel and dining and 1 "mile" per dollar on all other purchases, which is essentially 2% and 1% cash back on those purchases respectively. You get 25% more value (2.5% or 1.25%) when you use your points for booking airfare, hotels, rental cars, or cruises. The added 0.5% makes this a better card than our cashback cards for booking travel. Furthermore, this card grants 50,000 bonus miles or $625 once you've spent a minimum of $4,000 on purchases within three months of opening the card. Unless you travel often, it's likely this card is only worth using your first year since there is a $0 annual fee the first year but a $95 annual fee each year after the first.

Capital One Venture Rewards

The Capital One® Venture rewards Visa card[70] offers 2 "miles" per dollar on all purchases, which is essentially 2% cash back on *all* purchases and your rewards can be redeemed on travel related purchases such as airfare, hotels, rental cars, or cruises. While this is worse than our cashback cards, this card grants 40,000 miles or $400 once you've spent a minimum of $3,000 on purchases within three months of opening the card. This card is only worth using your first year since there is $0 annual fee the first year but a $59 annual fee each year after the first.

---

[68] https://www.capitalone.com/credit-cards/savor-dining-rewards/
[69] https://creditcards.chase.com/credit-cards/chase-sapphire-preferred2
[70] https://www.capitalone.com/credit-cards/venture/

Financial Priorities

1. Automate expense tracking and establish categorized budgets to control and predict your spending.
2. Project your finances to reveal the future impact of your spending and saving.
3. Save one month's income in an easily accessible checking account as a bank account buffer.
4. If your employer matches contributions to your 401(k), contribute up to the maximum match for free money and invest it in low fee global market stock portfolio and domestic bond funds, increasing bond allocation as you approach retirement.
5. Monitor and increase your credit score.
6. **Pay down credit card debt in order of descending interest rate while rotating balances over 0-interest cards.**
7. **Earn cashback rewards on your purchases.**

8.

Chapter 8 – Emergency Funds, Short-Term Goals, IRAs, and Taxable Accounts

Emergency Funds

You've already built a bank account buffer of one month's income in your checking account, but what if an emergency causes you to need more cash quickly? Your emergency fund is designed to provide you quick access to cash in case a medical problem, property damage, or job loss causes you to need unanticipated access to cash. The ability to have quick access to cash is a key tenant in Money Smartly's focus of "maximizing your net worth while *keeping your funds liquid*." While you could (if your 401(k) administrator allows it) borrow from your 401(k), you risk owing taxes and penalties on your loan if you are unable to pay the loan back with interest before the loan-repayment period or before leaving your employer, and sometimes your administrator won't allow you to contribute to your 401(k) before your loan is repaid. Therefore, other vehicles are more appropriate to house your emergency funds.

Many financial advisors recommend keeping three to six months' expenses in a checking or savings account as an emergency fund requirement. This is meant to cover most people's worst case scenario for finding another job in the case of a job loss. While the average job search takes just over six weeks according to a survey by Time Inc., other jobs including most high-level jobs can take longer and it varies by industry.[71] You should pick a number of months' expenses that makes you comfortable, but most people fall in the three to six months' range.

Investing Your Emergency Fund

While an emergency fund could be kept in a checking account or savings account where it's safe, this approach causes you to miss out on so much earning potential while there are higher earning means to keep your

---

[71] https://time.com/money/4053899/how-long-it-takes-to-get-hired/

emergency fund requirement safe. A six month emergency fund of $18,000 earning 1% in a savings account instead of investing it over the course of 30 years before retirement in stocks and bonds the way recommended in Chapter 5 – 401(k)s would cause you to miss out on over $110,000 of earnings!

To ensure your emergency fund is safe, I recommend doubling the size of your emergency fund—after subtracting the amount in your bank account buffer—to up to four to ten months' expenses (assuming your bank account buffer is at least one month's expenses) and investing it. I recommend doubling the invested portion of your emergency fund because a 50% market crash would cause those funds to fall back to your emergency fund requirement and a 50% market crash has happened only twice in history: the great depression and the great recession.[72] Even in those cases, it took more than a year for the markets to drop by 50%, which is time you could be using your income to build your emergency fund back up if you haven't already cashed it out to leverage it. Additionally, the majority of the time your invested emergency fund will be growing larger than your initial target, making this approach even safer.

[Target invested emergency fund amount] = 2 * ([Emergency fund requirement] – [Bank account buffer])

IRAs

The best place to invest an emergency fund is in an IRA or "Individual Retirement Account." They are similar to 401(k)s except that IRAs are offered by financial institutions rather than employers and you contribute directly with the financial institution. Traditional IRAs are tax-deferred accounts and Roth IRAs are tax-exempt accounts. When you contribute to a Traditional IRA, because the money isn't coming out of your paycheck before being taxed like it would in a Traditional 401(k), you instead write the contributions on your tax filings each year which will allow for an appropriate tax refund. In 2018 IRAs have a yearly cap of $5,500 with an additional $1,000 catch-up limit for those who are 50 or older and these

---

[72] http://www.nbcnews.com/id/37740147/ns/business-stocks_and_economy/t/historic-bear-markets/#.WZd6MFV96po

contribution limits apply in total over any number of Traditional IRAs and Roth IRAs you (not your spouse) contribute to. Furthermore, you can only contribute up to your taxable compensation for the year.[73]

Qualifying for Contributions and Tax Deductions

Traditional IRAs have a couple restrictions[74]:

- You must be under the age of 70 ½ (the age at which Uncle Sam requires people to cease making contributions and start making withdrawals from a Traditional IRA).
- You must have received taxable compensation such as wages from salary, self-employment, fees, tips, bonuses, commissions, or taxable alimony, in the year in which you are contributing to an IRA. Items that do not count as taxable compensation include pensions, retirement account distributions, Social Security benefits, interest and dividends from investments, unemployment benefits, and child support.

Even if you qualify, if and only if you or your spouse are covered by a workplace retirement plan such as a 401(k) or pension plan, Traditional IRAs have income limits that might prevent you from being able to deduct some or all of your IRA contributions off your taxes. You are considered "covered" by a workplace retirement plan as long as the plan is available for you to make contributions to, even if you opt not to make contributions. The income limits pertain to your "modified adjusted gross income," ("MAGI") which is approximately your income after subtracting contributions to Traditional 401(k)s (but not Roth). In 2018, that limit is $63,000 for single tax filers, $101,000 for married filing jointly (combined MAGI) tax filers, and $10,000 for married filing separately tax filers, and past those incomes your ability to deduct your contributions from taxes starts getting phased out.[75]

---

[73] https://www.irs.gov/newsroom/irs-announces-2018-pension-plan-limitations-401k-contribution-limit-increases-to-18500-for-2018

[74] https://www.fool.com/retirement/iras/2015/06/16/ira-eligibility-can-i-contribute-to-an-ira-in-2015.aspx

[75] https://www.irs.gov/retirement-plans/plan-participant-employee/2018-ira-contribution-and-deduction-limits-effect-of-modified-agi-on-deductible-contributions-if-you-are-covered-by-a-retirement-plan-at-work

If you have not received taxable earned income, but your spouse has, you are eligible to contribute to a Spousal Traditional IRA, but the rules differ[76]:

- For a spousal traditional IRA, you must be married, file a joint income tax return, and the household must have earned income of at least the total amount contributed to all IRAs (both spouses' IRAs). Also, the spousal IRA must be held in his or her name and tax identification number.

If your spouse participates in a workplace retirement plan, Spousal IRAs also have income limits that might prevent you from being able to deduct some or all your Spousal IRA contributions off your taxes. In 2018, that limit is $189,000. We'll review the income limits below.

Traditional IRA tax deductibility income limits if you **are** covered by a workplace retirement plan[77]:

If Your Filing Status Is...	**And Your Modified AGI Is...**	**Then You Can Take...**
single or **head of household**	$63,000 or less	a full deduction up to the amount of your contribution limit.
	more than $63,000 but less than $73,000	a partial deduction.
	$73,000 or more	no deduction.
married filing jointly or **qualifying widow(er)**	$101,000 or less	a full deduction up to the amount of your contribution limit.
	more than $101,000 but less than $121,000	a partial deduction.

[76] https://www.fool.com/retirement/iras/2015/06/16/ira-eligibility-can-i-contribute-to-an-ira-in-2015.aspx

[77] https://www.irs.gov/retirement-plans/plan-participant-employee/2016-ira-contribution-and-deduction-limits-effect-of-modified-agi-on-deductible-contributions-if-you-are-covered-by-a-retirement-plan-at-work

	$121,000 or more	no deduction.
married filing separately	less than $10,000	a partial deduction.
	$10,000 or more	no deduction.

Traditional IRA tax deductibility income limits if you **are not** covered by a workplace retirement plan[78]:

If Your Filing Status Is...	And Your Modified AGI Is...	Then You Can Take...
single, head of household, or qualifying widow(er)	any amount	a full deduction up to the amount of your contribution limit.
married filing jointly or separately with a spouse who is not covered by a plan at work	any amount	a full deduction up to the amount of your contribution limit.
married filing jointly with a spouse who is covered by a plan at work	$189,000 or less	a full deduction up to the amount of your contribution limit.
	more than $189,000 but less than $199,000	a partial deduction.
	$199,000 or more	no deduction.
married filing separately with a spouse who is covered by a plan at work	less than $10,000	a partial deduction.
	$10,000 or more	no deduction.

[78]https://www.irs.gov/retirement-plans/plan-participant-employee/2018-ira-contribution-and-deduction-limits-effect-of-modified-agi-on-deductible-contributions-if-you-are-not-covered-by-a-retirement-plan-at-work

Traditional IRAs, whether they are spousal or not, are like 401(k)s in that any withdrawal before the age of 59 ½ is subject to an additional 10% penalty on top of any taxes owed. There are a few exceptions including[79]:

- Un-reimbursed medical expenses
- Medical insurance
- Disability
- Higher education expenses
- First time home purchase
- A call to active duty

Unlike 401(k)s there are no IRA loans, only withdrawals. To allow for rollovers, IRA withdrawals can be repaid within 60 days before taxes or penalties apply. This can act as a short term loan where you withdraw from an IRA for up to 60 days and pay it back (even to the same IRA), but this is not recommended because of the tax and penalty consequences for not repaying within 60 days. You can only do this "rollover" once per calendar year.[80]

Roth IRAs

If your income (or if you don't work, your spouse's income) is above the limit at which tax deductibility starts being phased out, you might want to contribute to a Roth IRA. Even if your income is below the limit, if you determined a Roth 401(k) was advantageous for you over a Traditional 401(k), then you'll probably want to choose a Roth IRA over a Traditional IRA.

The rules are looser for Roth IRAs than they are for Traditional IRAs[81]:

- Unlike the rules that cut off traditional IRA eligibility at age 70 ½, the Roth IRA has no age restrictions.

---

[79] http://www.investopedia.com/articles/retirement/02/111202.asp
[80] http://finance.zacks.com/can-funds-taken-out-put-back-roth-ira-1292.html
[81] https://www.fool.com/retirement/iras/2015/06/16/ira-eligibility-can-i-contribute-to-an-ira-in-2015.aspx

- You must have received taxable compensation such as wages from salary, self-employment, fees, tips, bonuses, commissions, or taxable alimony, in the year in which you are contributing to a Roth IRA.
- For a spousal Roth IRA, you must be married and file a joint income tax return. The same eligibility rules for the working member of the household apply to the non-working spouse. Also, the spousal Roth IRA must be held in his or her name and tax identification number.
- In order to be eligible to contribute fully to a Roth IRA, your MAGI must be less than $120,000 for a single filer in 2018, and $189,000 or less for married filing jointly.[82]

Contributions to Roth IRAs are not subject to the 10% early withdrawal penalty even though any earnings are. This is why the government requires you to report your Roth IRA contributions in your tax filings each year because the sum of those contributions is the amount you're able to withdraw at any time for any reason without tax or penalty. Besides regular contributions, Roth IRAs can grow from rollover or conversion contributions such as a rollover from a Roth 401(k) after leaving an employer or a conversion of funds from a Traditional IRA to your Roth IRA. Money comes out of your Roth IRA in the following order and these rules dictate the liquidity of your assets[83]:

1. Regular contributions.
   a. Always tax- and penalty-free.
2. Rollover or conversion contributions from another account into a Roth IRA account.
   a. They come out on a first-in, first-out basis. Conversions from the earliest year come out first.
   b. Always tax-free.
   c. If the rollover or conversion caused you to pay tax on a portion of its funds, the portion you paid taxes on comes out of the Roth IRA first. This is intended to prevent people under age 59 ½ from converting a Traditional IRA to a Roth IRA and then immediately taking a distribution thereby circumventing the Traditional IRA early withdrawal penalty. To

[82] https://www.irs.gov/retirement-plans/plan-participant-employee/amount-of-roth-ira-contributions-that-you-can-make-for-2018
[83] https://www.irs.gov/publications/p590b/ch02.html

prevent the penalty, you must wait five years after the conversion to withdraw the funds.[84]

3. Earnings on contributions
   a. If withdrawn earlier than five years after your first Roth IRA account was initially funded:
      i. You pay tax (if under age 59 ½) and a 10% penalty on your earnings.
   b. If withdrawn at least five years after your first Roth IRA account was initially funded:
      i. You pay *only tax* (if under age 59 ½) on your earnings.[85]

The loose rules on contribution withdrawals for Roth IRAs allow you to use Roth IRA contributions (but not Traditional IRA contributions) as emergency funds. Furthermore, supplementing a Traditional 401(k) with a Roth IRA has the benefit of diversifying your savings and giving you the ability to control your tax bracket in retirement. By withdrawing less from your Traditional 401(k) in retirement and more from your Roth IRA to cover expenses, you can keep your income—withdrawals from your Traditional 401(k)—low enough to keep you in a low tax bracket. The five-year wait rule after a Roth IRA conversion provides a means to withdraw Traditional 401(k) or IRA funds prior to age 59 ½.

Backdoor Roth IRA

If your income is too high to be eligible to contribute to a Roth IRA, you should take advantage of the Backdoor Roth IRA option. A Backdoor Roth IRA is a means for high-income earners to contribute to a Traditional IRA and covert those funds to a Roth IRA. A Traditional IRA actually contains two buckets of money: before-tax and after-tax. All contributions that were eligible for tax deductions go into the before-tax bucket, whereas all contributions that were not go into the after-tax bucket. Unlike Roth conversions from before-tax buckets, after-tax bucket Roth conversions are not subject to taxes when converted since they were already taxed

---

[84] https://www.thebalance.com/the-scoop-on-roth-iras-are-withdrawals-tax-free-or-not-2388706

[85] https://www.hrblock.com/get-answers/taxes/taxes-and-penalties/early-withdrawal-penalties-10768

previously. Therefore, you can contribute funds to a Traditional IRA's after-tax bucket, convert them to a Roth IRA without triggering further taxes, and your funds will then generate earnings without capital gains tax drag and your converted amount can be withdrawn tax-free after five years and your earnings accrued while in the Roth IRA can be withdrawn tax-free after age 59 ½.[86]

Backdoor Roth IRA (for high income earners)

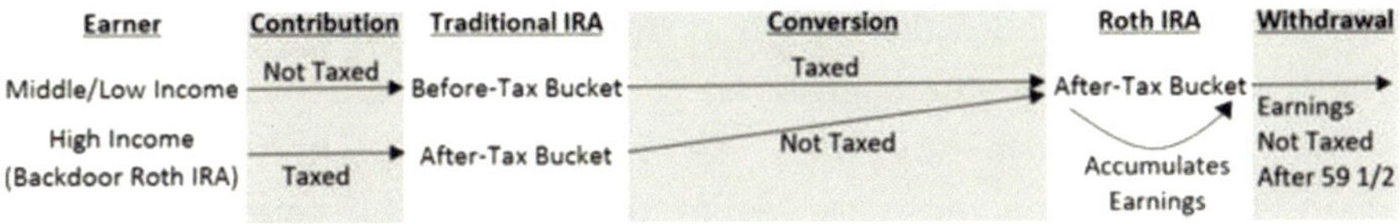

The Traditional IRA to Roth IRA conversion must be done correctly. Per the pro-rata rule, if you have pre-existing before-tax funds in any IRA account such as a Traditional IRA and you attempt to convert funds to a Roth IRA, a percentage of those funds equal to the percentage of all IRA funds that are before-tax will be taxable.[87] You can get around this by rolling over any funds in a Traditional IRA into an employer sponsored plan such as a 401(k), which doesn't count towards the pro-rata rule, before implementing the conversion to the Roth IRA.[88]

Mega Backdoor Roth IRA

There is a way for low- and high-income earners alike to contribute up to tens of thousands of dollars to a Roth IRA each year, but it requires your employer to offer a couple options through your 401(k):

1. Your employer must offer "non-Roth after-tax contributions" to your 401(k).
2. Best if your employer offers "in-service withdrawals."

---

[86] https://20somethingfinance.com/backdoor-roth-ira/
[87] https://www.irs.gov/retirement-plans/rollovers-of-after-tax-contributions-in-retirement-plans
[88] https://www08.wellsfargomedia.com/assets/pdf/personal/investing/retirement/taxes-and-retirement/pro-rata-rule.pdf

While you are limited to contributing $18,500 per year between your before-tax Traditional 401(k) and after-tax Roth 401(k), there is a third kind of contribution that's less talked-about called "non-Roth after-tax contributions" that go to an after-tax bucket of your Traditional 401(k), which is analogous to the after-tax bucket in a Traditional IRA. In 2018, you and your employer can contribute up to a combined $55,000 per year between all three 401(k) buckets: up to $18,500 between your Traditional 401(k) before-tax bucket and your Roth 401(k) after-tax bucket and the remainder ($36,500-$55,000) to your Traditional 401(k) after-tax bucket.[89] These non-Roth after-tax contributions are less talked-about because the earnings these contributions make are taxed as income when you withdraw them. Those income taxes are higher than the capital gains taxes those earnings would be subject to if you had invested in a taxable account, so why make these non-Roth after-tax contributions? Well, if your employer allows "in-service withdrawals," which are withdrawals from your account while you are working for your employer, then you can make these after-tax contributions, immediately or shortly-thereafter roll them over into your Roth IRA before much earnings accumulate, and now have those contributions accumulate earnings while they're in your Roth IRA where earnings are not subject to income *or* capital gains taxes after age 59 ½. This is sometimes referred to as the "Mega Backdoor Roth IRA." You can also access those rolled over contributions immediately without penalty due to the Roth IRA withdrawal order rules.

If your employer doesn't offer frequent in-service withdrawals, you can still do the Mega Backdoor Roth IRA, but since the earnings that accumulate from your non-roth after-tax contributions weren't taxed they will need to be rolled over to a Traditional IRA (and the contributions to a Roth IRA as before) once you leave your employer and so those earnings will be subject to income taxes once you roll them over from your Traditional IRA into your Roth IRA.[90] While you can still access the original contributions immediately without penalty, due to the Roth IRA withdrawal order rules you must wait five years to access the earnings without penalty. If you stay with your

---

[89] https://www.irs.gov/newsroom/irs-announces-2018-pension-plan-limitations-401k-contribution-limit-increases-to-18500-for-2018

[90] https://www.irs.gov/retirement-plans/rollovers-of-after-tax-contributions-in-retirement-plans

employer for short enough a period, you can still come out ahead with a Mega Backdoor Roth IRA, but I do not recommend using a Mega Backdoor Roth IRA unless your employer allows you to withdraw in-service at least once a year since capital gains taxes are much easier to avoid than income taxes.

Mega Backdoor Roth IRA

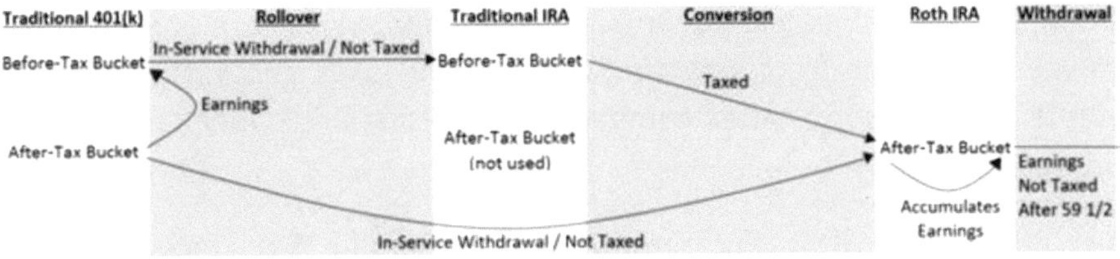

Contributing to Your Emergency Fund

In 1975, under the premise that investors as a whole can't outperform the market because they *are* the market and so the ideal fund would provide broad diversification at extraordinarily low cost, John Bogle founded the Vanguard 500 Index Fund as the first index mutual fund available to the general public. Index funds are designed to match the market's returns without need for expensive active management of the fund. Bogle created the Vanguard Group, now the largest provider of mutual funds in the world, with his 8-rule approach to investing:

1. Select low-cost funds.
2. Consider carefully the added costs of advice.
3. Do not overrate past fund performance.
4. Use past performance to determine consistency and risk.
5. Beware of stars (as in, star mutual fund managers).
6. Beware of asset size.
7. Don't own too many funds.
8. Buy your fund portfolio—and hold it.

Vanguard has a unique company structure in that the company is owned by its funds and its funds are owned by its shareholders such that there are no outside owners looking to make profits from the funds' fees. There are other companies such as Schwab and Fidelity that offer a limited number of basic index funds at minimally lower fees than Vanguard as loss leaders, but the breadth of low fee funds available at Vanguard makes them my financial institution of choice.[91] If you start investing in a taxable account, you may want to leverage these other Vanguard funds for "tax loss harvesting," which we'll cover later in this chapter. Furthermore, Vanguard has patented their "share-class ETFs" where their mutual fund and ETF assets of the same index are pooled together, providing the mutual fund more assets to harvest tax losses from, slightly lowering the taxes generated from the mutual fund, and no other company can do this until Vanguard's patent expires in 2021.[92]

Just like your 401(k) allocation, you need a fund that tracks domestic markets, a fund that tracks international markets, and a fund that tracks US bond markets. Vanguard funds require a minimum investment of $3,000.Just as we stated in Chapter 5 – 401(k)s, you should allocate 42% of your stock allocation to a domestic fund such as the Vanguard Total Stock Market Index Fund, 58% of your stock allocation to an international fund such as the Vanguard Total International Stock Index Fund, and your bond allocation to a bond fund such as the Vanguard Intermediate-Term Treasury Fund in an IRA or the Vanguard Intermediate-Term Tax-Exempt Fund in taxable accounts. The table below shows an example allocation, the tickers for the funds and their associated fees ("expense ratio").

Allocation	Fund Name	Mutual Fund (ER)
33.3%	Vanguard Total Stock Market Index Fund	VTSAX (0.04%)
45.9%	Vanguard Total International Stock Index Fund	VTIAX (0.11%)
8.1%	Vanguard Real Estate Index Fund	VGSLX (0.12%)
2.7%	Vanguard Small-Cap Value Index Fund	VSIAX (0.07%)
0-10%	Vanguard Intermediate-Term Treasury Fund (Tax-Advantaged Accounts)	VSIGX (0.07%)
0-10%	Vanguard Intermediate-Term Tax-Exempt Fund (Taxable Accounts)*	VWITX (0.19%) or VWIUX (0.09%)**

[91] https://www.schwabfunds.com/public/file/P-10043741
[92] https://advisors.vanguard.com/iwe/pdf/standAloneTrans.pdf

* If you live in California, Massachusetts, New Jersey, New York, Ohio, or Pennsylvania there are alternative Vanguard funds you should use in taxable accounts to exempt earnings from specific state income taxes.
** Requires minimum $50,000 investment.

If you are just starting out investing and you don't have enough money to meet Vanguard's balance minimums while adhering to your allocation, I recommend opening an account with Betterment.com. Betterment is one of the new online fully automated investment advisers which are often referred to as "robo-advisors." You tell Betterment what your target stock/bond allocation percentage is as well as how much you want to transfer from your checking account now and each month to invest and they handle the rest. Betterment will invest your money into index funds comprised mostly of Vanguard funds for a reasonable fee of 0.25% in addition to the fund fees. The advantage with investing in Betterment is that they don't have any investment minimum so you can invest with them until you have enough money to meet Vanguard's investment minimums and then roll over your funds from Betterment into a Vanguard IRA or taxable account to eliminate the additional 0.25% fee.

Saving For Your Emergency Fund and Other Priorities

If it'll take you awhile to save four to ten months' expenses as an emergency fund, you should build it up in your checking account or a high-yield savings account such as Ally.com[93] to protect it from losses, but once it reaches your required three to six months' expenses, start investing any new savings and an equivalent amount from your checking or savings account into a Roth IRA or taxable investment account until your checking account is left with only your bank account buffer. For example, if your monthly expenses are $2,000 and you have your desired three month $6,000 emergency fund in your checking account and you have an additional $250 of income to contribute to your emergency fund each month, you should invest the $250 income and an additional $250 from your checking or savings account into a Roth IRA or taxable investment account each month until your checking account only has one month's income (your bank account buffer) remaining. This has the benefit of keeping your emergency fund safe as the portion in the

---

[93] https://www.ally.com/bank/online-savings-account/

checking account experiences no volatility and the portion in the Roth IRA or taxable account is padded to minimize the risk from volatility.

After saving up an emergency fund, you are considered financially secure and can begin saving for any short-term goals. If you are looking to save for a wedding or down payment on a house or car within the next five years, that money should be saved in the same manner as your emergency fund: start saving in a checking or high-yield savings account until reaching your goal then match additional savings from income with money from your checking or savings account and invest it in a Roth IRA or taxable investment account until it reaches double the amount of your goal. Be sure to not consider your emergency funds as the same funds for your short-term goals.

Extending the Life of Your Emergency Fund

You can often extend the life of your emergency fund through 0% interest rate credit cards. If you apply for 0% interest rate credit cards after losing your job and use them for purchases up to their credit limit while using your emergency fund to make their minimum monthly payments, you can extend your emergency fund by several months while you search for a job to pay those credit card balances down before they start accruing interest. Credit card companies often provide high-credit customers blank checks in the mail with 0% interest and a low 2-4% upfront fee which are also decent options for extending your emergency fund's life.

Managing Investments

Dollar Cost Averaging

While most of the time people contribute a set amount of their income to their IRAs and taxable investment accounts monthly, you may come across a lump sum of money that you're looking to invest. If you invest that lump sum all at once you risk investing it when the market is high only to see the market fall shortly thereafter. To avoid this risk, you can dollar cost average your investment, which is the practice of spreading your lump sum investment into a number of smaller investments over time.

Over what period of time should you spread your investments over? Dr. Bill Jones studied this issue and found that the length depends on the percentage of assets you are investing because the more you invest the more inclined you should be to manage risk by spreading out contributions over a longer timeframe.[94] He found that any sum less than 5% of your assets should be invested over no more than 6 months, any sum between 5% and 30% of your assets should be invested over no more than 12 months, and any sum greater than 30% of your assets should be invested over no more than 18 months. Note that since the market always has a positive expectation in theory, dollar cost averaging never maximizes your return, but this is a good guideline in how short period dollar cost averaging can reasonably minimize your risk due to volatile markets. Better yet, you could invest the lump sum in bonds first and slowly transfer it to stocks over this dollar cost averaging period.

Tax Efficient Asset Placement

If you are utilizing taxable investment accounts in addition to tax-advantaged investment accounts, placing tax-efficient funds in your taxable account and tax-inefficient funds in your tax-advantaged accounts can reduce your tax drag by an additional 0.10% - 0.82% per year according to Betterment, which after 30 years can grow your investments by 15% more than they otherwise would have grown.[95] In general, real estate and bond funds are the least tax-efficient funds since they produce dividends taxed as income. Next, stock funds with high "turnover rate" such as active funds that frequently sell stock shares realize more capital gains tax than passive index funds. Of passive index funds, funds tilted towards value stocks tend to be less tax-efficient than growth tilted funds because value stocks often grant their shareholders dividends. Lastly, if those dividends aren't qualified as is often the case with international funds, then the dividends will be taxed at the higher short term capital gains rates (same as income tax rates).

Taxes generated from international funds also come with a "foreign tax credit" where the U.S. government credits your taxes to offset your double

[94] http://www.efficientfrontier.com/ef/997/dca.htm
[95] https://www.betterment.com/resources/research/tax-coordinated-portfolio-white-paper/

taxation (taxed both by foreign countries and by the U.S.). Technically those in the 24% tax bracket or lower tend to favor international index funds in their taxable account since they are taxed low on non-qualified dividends and can then claim the foreign tax credit for a net gain; whereas those in the 32% tax bracket or higher tend to favor domestic index funds in their taxable account since they are taxed high on non-qualified dividends and the foreign tax credit usually doesn't fully offset those taxes.

In summary, first place as much of your real estate then bond funds into your 401(k) or IRAs as possible, then fill up the remaining room with your domestic (for lower tax brackets) or international (for higher tax brackets) funds. Be sure this doesn't cause you to pick a 401(k) fund with a high expense ratio as the higher fees might eliminate the benefit tax-efficient asset placement provides. If you must put some bonds into your taxable account, it's advantageous to use municipal bonds, which are tax exempt and tend to yield less before-tax return but greater after-tax return than other bond funds.

Tax Loss Harvesting

For funds in taxable accounts, you can take action to minimize taxes owed. "Tax loss harvesting" is the practice of selling a fund which has experienced a capital loss to offset the amount of realized capital gains investors must claim on their taxes. According to Betterment, tax loss harvesting can yield a portfolio an additional 0.77% per year.[96] You would first use any losses (whether short term or long term capital losses) to offset short term capital gains since they are taxed higher as income. Next, if you have remaining losses, you would use them to offset long term capital gains. Lastly, if you harvest more capital losses than you had capital gains to offset, you can then use any remaining tax losses to deduct up to $3,000 from your regular income taxes each year, saving you up to $660 in taxes if you're in the 22% tax bracket. If and only if you still have additional losses without remaining capital gains or income to offset, you can roll the remaining losses over to offset next year's capital gains and income in the same order.[97] In order to maximize losses to harvest, you must sell the particular shares you bought

[96] https://www.betterment.com/tax-loss-harvesting/
[97] https://personal.vanguard.com/pdf/s802.pdf

at the highest price. Most investment companies, including Vanguard, allow you to select particular shares to sell using a cost basis method known as "specific identification."

When harvesting losses, investors typically replace the sold fund by buying a similar fund with the money earned from the sale, maintaining their asset allocation and expected returns. The table below shows what similar fund you can buy in favoring of harvesting tax losses for each of the funds we previously recommended (besides the REIT fund as it should always be held in a tax-advantaged account).

Fund	Mutual Fund	Similar Fund	Mutual Fund
Total Stock Market Index	VTSAX (0.04%)	500 Index	VFIAX (0.04%)
Total International Stock Index	VTIAX (0.11%)	FTSE All-World Ex-US	VFWAX (0.11%)
Small-Cap Value Index	VSIAX (0.07%)	Mid-Cap Value Index	VMVAX (0.07%)
Intermediate-Term Treasury Fund	VSIGX (0.07%)	Intermediate-Term Bond Index	VBIRX (0.07%)
Intermediate-Term Tax-Exempt Fund*	VWITX (0.19) or VWIUX** (0.09)	Limited-Term Tax-Exempt Fund	VMLTX (0.19%) or VMLUX** (0.09%)

* If you live in California, Massachusetts, New Jersey, New York, Ohio, or Pennsylvania there are alternative Vanguard funds you should use in taxable accounts to exempt earnings from state income taxes.

** Requires minimum $50,000 investment.

When harvesting losses, you must be sure to avoid any illegal "wash sales," which is the practice of taking a tax loss harvest on a fund in a taxable account and buying that fund or a substantially similar fund back in a taxable account or IRA (401(k)s aren't subject to this rule) within 30 days. The IRS hasn't been very specific in what constitutes a substantially similar fund, but it's widely considered safe to buy a fund tracking a different index than the index of the fund you sold. Betterment will automatically avoid wash sales for you, so make sure you rollover any IRAs to Betterment before enabling Tax Loss Harvesting. Vanguard won't avoid wash sales for you, so be sure to turn off automatically reinvesting dividends and after harvesting losses, adjust your monthly automated transfer to either be at least 31 days later or to invest in your new alternate fund for just your next transfer.

Financial Priorities

1. Automate expense tracking and establish categorized budgets to control and predict your spending.
2. Project your finances to reveal the future impact of your spending and saving.
3. Save one month's income in an easily accessible checking account as a bank account buffer.
4. If your employer matches contributions to your 401(k), contribute up to the maximum match for free money and invest it in low fee global market stock portfolio and domestic bond funds, increasing bond allocation as you approach retirement.
5. Monitor and increase your credit score.
6. Pay down credit card debt in order of descending interest rate while rotating balances over 0-interest cards.
7. Earn cashback rewards on your purchases.
8. **Subtract your bank account bufferfrom your desired emergency fund and invest twice that amount for up to four to ten months' expenses in a Roth IRA up to the max (through a Backdoor Roth IRA or Mega Backdoor Roth IRA if necessary) then a taxable investment account for a safe, high-earning emergency fund.**
9. **Start saving for any short term goals such as a wedding or down payment on a house in a savings account until reaching your goal then match additional savings from income with money from your savings account and invest it in a Roth IRA up to the max (through a Backdoor Roth IRA or Mega Backdoor Roth IRA if necessary and available) then a taxable investment account until it reaches double the amount of your goal. Utilize tax loss harvesting and tax efficient asset placement to minimize your taxable investment account's taxes.**

Chapter 9 – Health Insurance

While emergency funds cover reasonably affordable emergencies, rare emergencies such as health care emergencies can be so expensive we need a plan B to cover them. Plan B is insurance. Insurance companies make their money by charging customers more than they are likely to receive back in insurance claims. That said, insurance is a necessity to protect you from financial ruin in case of an unaffordable disaster. This means the best approach to insurance is to take out as little of it as you would be able to reasonably afford if a disaster were to happen. High deductibles come with low premiums. Unless your employer pays your health insurance premiums, it is a good strategy to sign up for a health insurance plan with a deductible and out-of-pocket maximum as high as your emergency fund requirement minus one month's income to preserve your bank account buffer.

High Deductible Health Plans

Plans that are marked as HDHP (High Deductible Health Plans) are plans with deductibles above a certain limit, which in 2018 is $1,350 for self-coverage or $2,700 for family-coverage. If you're enrolled in one of these plans, you are eligible to contribute to an HSA (Health Savings Account) which is an investment account designed to incentivize you to save money in case you need that money to cover medical expenses.

HSAs are also one of the best investment vehicles in existence because they are tax-exempt, so you don't pay taxes on money put into the account, and tax-free and penalty-free when used for medical expenses, so you don't pay taxes when taking money out of the account to cover medical expenses. This is the only long-term investment vehicle where you can avoid income taxes completely and not just capital gains taxes. If you withdraw money for non-medical purposes a 20% penalty applies in addition to taxes, but after age 65 non-medical withdrawals are penalty-free (but not tax-free). This means that even if you don't take advantage of your HSA's "triple tax savings" on medical expenses, it effectively acts as an additional Traditional IRA. If you are in the 22% tax bracket, your HSA contributions can save you up to $759 per year as an individual and up to $1,518 per year as a family on current or future qualified medical expenses.

Many employers will even contribute to an HSA on your behalf or match your contributions which like a 401(k) match is another free money scenario. In 2018 the max HSA contribution limit is $3,450 for self-coverage and $6,900 for family-coverage and unlike Traditional or Roth 401(k) contribution limits, this limit takes into account both what you contribute and what your employer contributes combined. Similar to an IRA, you may contribute $1,000 extra per year if you are 55 or older as a catch-up contribution.[98]

Contributions to HSAs are your highest financial priority *if* your employer matches those contributions. After taking advantage of all employer matches to your HSA and 401(k), you should save up to your expected yearly medical expenses in your HSA to make those expenses effectively cheaper. Any additional HSA contributions come after saving for important short-term goals.

If you've already reached your target liquid savings for your short-term goals, you can really start taking advantage of an HSA provision that boosts long-term savings. Nothing in the HSA law prohibits expensing previous years' expenses. The only limit is that the expenses must have occurred after you setup your first HSA. Therefore, once you're ready to accumulate long-term savings, in addition to maxing out your HSA you should start using liquid savings in lieu of HSA funds to pay medical expenses and save all your medical receipts because HSA funds will experience compounding earnings without tax-drag while in the HSA, then in late retirement you can withdraw the total of your expenses from previous years' medical receipts from your HSA tax-free.

While the advantages of HSAs are great, it's not a substitute for cheap low-deductible health care provided by an employer. If signing up for a HDHP does not save you money in premiums and your employer does not contribute to your HSA, then it makes more sense to keep your deductible low for a better health insurance plan even though you cannot contribute to a HSA.

---

[98] https://www.irs.gov/pub/irs-drop/rp-17-37.pdf

Contributing to HSAs

Oftentimes your employer chooses what institution administers your HSA. If you can choose, one of the best administrators is HSABank.com due to their low fees and availability to all funds—including low fee Vanguard funds—on TD Ameritrade. If you keep your HSA cash balance at $5,000 or above, you can keep your HSA without them charging any fees. However, a benefit of a HSA is that you can invest the balance in stocks and bonds. Some HSA Bank customers hold a balance of $5,000 in their cash balance to avoid these fees; however, I don't advise this since that $5,000 would earn $300 per year when invested with a 6% return which is much higher than the $5.50 per month or $66 per year they'd charge you for having a cash balance below $5,000.

HSA Bank allows you to invest in a TD Ameritrade brokerage account which will only charge you for setting up your initial investments. I recommend paying their one-time $25 per fund fee to setup automated investments after each paycheck to allocate percentages into your funds of choice. An HSA is a tax-advantaged account and therefore a good option to hold real estate or bond index funds as mentioned in Chapter 8 – Emergency Funds, Short-Term Goals, IRAs, and Taxable Accounts. This one-time per fund fee will automate your investments with minimal fees from low fund expense ratios thereafter. Once setup, additional transactions between these funds are free.

Flexible Spending Accounts

Another account designed to incentivize you to save money for healthcare expenses is an FSA (Flexible Spending Account). FSAs are similar to HSAs in that contributions are tax-deferred and tax-free for medical expenses. What makes FSAs worse than HSAs is their "use it or lose it" policy. Some FSAs have a $500/year rollover so that you only lose the balance in excess of $500 at each year's end; whereas other FSAs have a 2 ½ month grace period after each year in which you can spend the remaining FSA balance.[99] Unlike HSAs, FSAs are associated with your employer such that you can't take your

[99] https://www.treasury.gov/press-center/press-releases/Documents/103113FSA%20Fact%20Sheet.pdf

balance with you when you leave your job. Due to the ability to lose your money, FSAs are only useful for setting aside money for medical expenses you are highly certain will occur. Other than that, I cannot recommend contributing to an FSA.

Affordable Care Act and Medicaid

The Affordable Care Act (a.k.a. "ACA" or "Obamacare") allows anyone to buy health insurance through HealthCare.gov. If your income is 400% of the federal poverty limit or lower, you will also get a tax credit (subsidy) equal to the difference between a percentage of your income (ranging from 2% - 9.5% shown in the table below) and the second cheapest ACA Silver plan available to your state.[100]

Number of Persons in Household	2018 Federal Poverty Limit
1	$12,060
2	$16,240
3	$20,420
4	$24,600
More	add $4,180 each

Note: Alaska and Hawaii have higher Federal Poverty Limits.[101]

Income as % of Federal Poverty Limit	Cap % (Lower End)	Cap % (Higher End)
100% - 133%	2.00%	2.00%
133% - 150%	3.00%	4.00%
150% - 200%	4.00%	6.30%
200% - 250%	6.30%	8.05%
250% - 300%	8.05%	9.50%
300% - 400%	9.50%	9.50%

The ACA requires insurers to categorize plans into 4 metal tiers upon how much of the policyholder's total health care costs the plan will cover. These metal tiers are Bronze, Silver, Gold, and Platinum with Bronze plans covering the least amount and Platinum plans covering the most. If the

[100] https://www.valuepenguin.com/understanding-aca-subsidies
[101] https://thefinancebuff.com/federal-poverty-levels-for-obamacare.html

Silver plan costs more than what your premium cap would be based upon your MAGI and your cap percentage, the government gives you a tax credit equal to the difference, which you can apply to an ACA plan of any metal tier, but if the plan you choose is cheaper than your subsidy you would lose the amount of the subsidy in excess of the cost of that plan. Note that this subsidy has a hard MAGI cliff at 400% the federal poverty limit and having a MAGI of one dollar more makes you ineligible for any subsidy. As such, if you enroll in ACA and are near the 400% limit, there is incentive to reduce your MAGI through means such as contributing to a Traditional 401(k).[102]

If your MAGI is 138% or less of the federal poverty limit, you might not qualify for an ACA subsidy, but you might qualify for Medicaid. Medicaid is a joint federal and state program that provides free or low-cost health coverage. Along with the ACA legislation came an option for states to expand Medicaid to cover those making too little to qualify for an ACA subsidy. As of early 2018, Washington D.C. and 32 states have accepted this Medicaid expansion. The remaining 18 states provide coverage for low MAGI, but unfortunately there may be a gap between the maximum MAGI to qualify for the state's Medicaid coverage and minimum MAGI (100% of the federal poverty limit) to qualify for ACA subsidies.[103] The Medicaid expansion income limit is stated as 133% of the federal poverty limit but it also allows you to deduct 5% of your MAGI from the calculation effectively making the Medicaid maximum 138% of the federal poverty limit.[104] The HealthCare.gov site will check if you qualify for Medicaid and will direct you to enroll in your state's Medicaid program if appropriate.

Financial Priorities

1. Automate expense tracking and establish categorized budgets to control and predict your spending.
2. Project your finances to reveal the future impact of your spending and saving.

---

[102] https://www.valuepenguin.com/understanding-aca-subsidies
[103] https://www.medicaid.gov/medicaid/program-information/medicaid-and-chip-eligibility-levels/
[104] http://www.shadac.org/news/aca-note-when-133-equals-138-fpl-calculations-affordable-care-act

3. Save one month's income in an easily accessible checking account as a bank account buffer.
4. **Sign up for a HSA if a High Deductible Health Plan saves you premiums or your employer contributes to your Health Savings Account. Contribute up to your employer's maximum match for free money in this HSA. If your employer's HSA match percentage is lower than their 401(k) match percentage, max out your 401(k) match before maxing out your HSA match.**
5. If your employer matches contributions to your 401(k), contribute up to the maximum match for free money and invest it in low fee global market stock portfolio and domestic bond funds, increasing bond allocation as you approach retirement.
6. **Save up to your expected yearly medical expenses in a HSA if you are covered by a High Deductible Health Plan for triple tax-free medical expenses.**
7. Monitor and increase your credit score.
8. Pay down credit card debt in order of descending interest rate while rotating balances over 0-interest cards.
9. Earn cashback rewards on your purchases.
10. Subtract your bank account buffer from your desired emergency fund and invest twice that amount for up to four to ten months' expenses in a Roth IRA up to the max (through a Backdoor Roth IRA or Mega Backdoor Roth IRA if necessary) then a taxable investment account for a safe, high-earning emergency fund.
11. Start saving for any short term goals such as a wedding or down payment on a house in a savings account until reaching your goal then match additional savings from income with money from your savings account and invest it in a Roth IRA up to the max (through a Backdoor Roth IRA or Mega Backdoor Roth IRA if necessary and available) then a taxable investment account until it reaches double the amount of your goal. Utilize tax loss harvesting and tax efficient asset placement to minimize your taxable investment account's taxes.

Chapter 10 – Saving For Your Future

After you've built your emergency fund and have saved for your current short-term goals, you can continue investing for your future. There are two approaches to investing for your future: optimizing your savings for retirement or efficiently investing liquid savings. The truth is that most of us will not save enough money in our careers to retire comfortably. In 2014 the median household income of middle-income households was $72,919[105] and the average savings rate was less than 6% of income.[106] Over a 40-year career that income and savings rate would result in less than $175,000 saved. Assuming a 4% safe withdrawal rate to last a 30 year retirement, $175,000 of savings would provide only $7,000 per year to live on! If you take those same savings and invest them for retirement you will have a much more reasonable $32,000 per year to live on. Clearly some of our savings must be invested for retirement, but how much?

Optimizing Savings For Retirement

The percentage of income that must be reserved for retirement depends on how much longer you want to work. Below is a table showing savings rate as a percentage of your gross income minus taxes and associated working years until you can retire while maintaining your standard of living, starting from a net worth of $0.[107]

Savings Rate	Working Years Until Retirement
5%	66
10%	51
15%	43
20%	37
25%	32

[105] https://www.cnbc.com/2017/03/24/heres-how-much-money-middle-class-families-earn-in-every-us-state.html
[106] https://ycharts.com/indicators/personal_saving_rate
[107] http://www.mrmoneymustache.com/2012/01/13/the-shockingly-simple-math-behind-early-retirement/

30%	28
35%	25
40%	22
45%	19
50%	17
55%	14.5
60%	12.5
65%	10.5
70%	8.5
75%	7
80%	5.5
85%	4
90%	under 3
95%	under 2
100%	zero

As you probably don't want to work for more than 43 years, the absolute minimum savings you should reserve for retirement is 15% of your gross income minus taxes per year. If you choose to reserve more savings for retirement, you are buying your way to "financial independence" and can take better advantage of tax-efficient savings vehicles.

The best vehicle to save for retirement is an HSA because you always avoid taxes when you contribute and you also avoid taxes when you withdraw for health related expenses. After maxing out your HSA, you need to decide which is better for you: saving on taxes now in traditional retirement accounts or saving on taxes in the future in roth retirement accounts. Most people will find traditional retirement accounts more attractive as they allow them to avoid income taxes now while they have less control over their income and still avoid income taxes in retirement when they have more control over their income (the amount they withdraw from these retirement accounts). Lastly, IRAs are typically better than 401(k)s because 401(k)s limit your investment options and oftentimes come with higher fees than you can find for your IRAs. The lists below show the investing priority order to follow:

If you favor traditional accounts (recommended for most people):

1. Max out your HSA.
2. Max out your Traditional IRA.
    a. Do this only if you qualify for Traditional IRA tax deductions.
3. Max out your 401(k).
    a. Assuming your employer offers one.
4. Max out your Roth IRA (through a backdoor Roth IRA if necessary).
    a. Added in case you do not qualify for Traditional IRA tax deductions.
5. Max out your Mega Backdoor Roth IRA
    a. Assuming your employer offers the requirements.
6. Contribute to a taxable investment account.

If you favor roth accounts:

1. Max out your HSA.
2. Max out your Roth IRA (through a backdoor Roth IRA if necessary).
3. Max out your Roth 401(k).
    a. Assuming your employer offers one.
    b. Your Roth 401(k) comes before your Mega Backdoor Roth IRA in case the later experiences any time lapses between contribution and in-service withdrawal, causing earnings to be taxed.
4. Max out your Mega Backdoor Roth IRA.
    a. Assuming your employer offers the requirements.
5. Max out your 401(k).
    a. Added in case your employer offers a traditional but not a roth 401(k) nor the requirements necessary to max out a Mega Backdoor Roth IRA.
6. Contribute to a taxable investment account.

Efficiently Investing Liquid Savings

If you've met your desired retirement savings and feel other matters are prioritized over your financial independence, you can start investing in an efficient—albeit less efficient than retirement savings—and liquid manner. If you feel you might want (but won't need) the money within 5 years, you should take a similar approach of saving for short term goals like we discussed in Chapter 8 – Emergency Funds, Short-Term Goals, IRAs, and Taxable Accounts: save the money in a Roth IRA (via Backdoor or Mega Backdoor Roth IRA if necessary and available), followed by a taxable account. This approach is a bit more risky than proposed for saving for short-term goals because it doesn't involve saving in a savings account first, but since you won't *need* this money, that is acceptable. If you believe you won't want the money until you leave your current employer, but you might want it before retirement, you can take advantage of a Roth 401(k) if your employer offers it. Roth 401(k) accounts don't allow for in-service withdrawals, but after you leave your employer you can roll it into your Roth IRA and can withdraw your basis penalty free. Your basis is the amount you contributed to the Roth 401(k) and if you contributed to your Roth IRA at least five years ago, your Roth 401(k) earnings become your basis as well![108] The list below shows the investing priority to follow:

1. Max out your Roth IRA (through a backdoor Roth IRA if necessary).
2. Max out your Mega Backdoor Roth IRA.
   a. Assuming your employer offers the requirements.
3. Max out your Roth 401(k).
   a. Assuming your employer offers one and you won't want the money until after you leave your employer.
4. Contribute to a taxable investment account.

Financial Priorities

1. Automate expense tracking and establish categorized budgets to control and predict your spending.
2. Project your finances to reveal the future impact of your spending and saving.
3. Save one month's income in an easily accessible checking account as a bank account buffer.
4. Sign up for a HSA if a High Deductible Health Plan saves you premiums or your employer contributes to your Health Savings Account. Contribute up to your employer's maximum match for free money in this HSA. If your employer's HSA match percentage is lower than their 401(k) match percentage, max out your 401(k) match before maxing out your HSA match.

---

[108] http://fairmark.com/retirement/roth-accounts/designated-roth-accounts/rollovers-from-designated-roth-accounts/

5. If your employer matches contributions to your 401(k), contribute up to the maximum match for free money and invest it in low fee global market stock portfolio and domestic bond funds, increasing bond allocation as you approach retirement.
6. Save up to your expected yearly medical expenses in a HSA if you are covered by a High Deductible Health Plan for triple tax-free medical expenses.
7. Monitor and increase your credit score.
8. Pay down credit card debt in order of descending interest rate while rotating balances over 0-interest cards.
9. Earn cashback rewards on your purchases.
10. Subtract your bank account buffer from your desired emergency fund and invest twice that amount for up to four to ten months' expenses in a Roth IRA up to the max (through a Backdoor Roth IRA or Mega Backdoor Roth IRA if necessary) then a taxable investment account for a safe, high-earning emergency fund.
11. Start saving for any short term goals such as a wedding or down payment on a house in a savings account until reaching your goal then match additional savings from income with money from your savings account and invest it in a Roth IRA up to the max (through a Backdoor Roth IRA or Mega Backdoor Roth IRA if necessary and available) then a taxable investment account until it reaches double the amount of your goal. Utilize tax loss harvesting and tax efficient asset placement to minimize your taxable investment account's taxes.
12. **Buy your financial independence by saving a target percentage of your gross income minus taxes (minimum 15%) to retire by your desired date and invest it in a tax optimal manner among your HSA, IRAs, 401(k)s, and taxable investment account. Stop using HSA funds to cover medical expenses, leaving HSA funds to compound earnings without tax-drag, and save medical receipts for future tax-free HSA withdrawals.**
13. **If you want to invest for future pre-retirement spending instead of using all your savings to buy financial independence, invest further savings in a tax efficient manner among your Roth IRA, Roth 401(k), and taxable investment account.**

Chapter 11 – 529 Plans

529 Plans are tax-advantaged vehicles to save for your children's college expenses. Money in a 529 can be withdrawn tax-free to cover tuition and room and board even for off-campus housing up to the cost of the room and board allowance determined by the college or university.[109] Like other tax-exempt accounts, you save by being exempt from capital gains tax. Contributions are made after taxes and therefore have no income tax advantages.

The disadvantage of 529 plans is that when funds are withdrawn for purposes other than educational expenses, earnings (not contributions) are subject to income tax instead of the capital gains tax they would be subject to for taxable accounts and an additional 10% penalty. An exception to the 10% penalty is when your child gets a scholarship—whether needs-based or merit-based—you can withdraw the amount of the scholarship from the 529 penalty-free, but the earnings, determined as the percent of your portfolio that is earnings multiplied by the withdrawal amount, will still be subject to incometax.[110] Furthermore, unlike funds in retirement accounts, funds in a 529 plan are counted as parental assets that hurt your child's eligibility for need based financial aid.

Financial Aid

The two major financial aid forms are the FAFSA and CSS Profile. Most colleges require the FAFSA to apply for federal financial aid; however, around 200 of the most well-known colleges in the country also require the CSS Profile to assess the student's eligibility for the college's own institutional aid dollars. The CSS Profile generally counts more assets than the FAFSA and reveals more about the family's true financial standing. However, with both forms, there are ways to secure your assets from being

---

[109] https://www.usnews.com/education/best-colleges/paying-for-college/articles/2015/06/17/4-common-questions-about-spending-529-college-savings-funds

[110] http://www.savingforcollege.com/articles/the-truth-about-scholarships-and-529-plans-880

counted and therefore increase the amount of financial aid your child can receive.

The forms take your household income and assets and calculate an Expected Family Contribution (EFC), which is the minimum amount your family is expected to contribute to the cost of your child's education. To start, there is an Income Protection Allowance and an Asset Protection Allowance that allows you to subtract a base amount of income and assets from counting against your child's eligibility for financial aid. The Income Protection Allowance increases with the number of people in your household and decreases with the number of those people who are students. The table below shows the Income Protection Allowance for the 2016-2017 school year.[111]

Table A3: Income Protection Allowance

Number in parents' household, including student (FAFSA/SAR #73)	Number of college students in the household (FAFSA/SAR #74)				
	1	2	3	4	5
2	$17,840	$14,790	not applicable	not applicable	not applicable
3	$22,220	$19,180	$16,130	not applicable	not applicable
4	$27,440	$24,390	$21,350	$18,300	not applicable
5	$32,380	$29,320	$26,290	$23,240	$20,200
6	$37,870	$34,820	$31,780	$28,730	$25,690

Note: For each additional family member, add $4,270.
For each additional college student (except parents), subtract $3,040.

After adjusting for this Income Protection Allowance, you can calculate an Adjusted Available Income (AAI) to find how much your income contributes to your EFC. The maximum is 47%, but the table below shows more brackets.[112]

[111] https://studentaid.ed.gov/sa/sites/default/files/2016-17-efc-formula.pdf
[112] https://studentaid.ed.gov/sa/sites/default/files/2016-17-efc-formula.pdf

Table A6: Parents' Contribution from AAI	
If the parents' AAI—	**Then the parents' contribution from AAI is—**
Less than -$3,409	-$750
$-3,409 to $15,900	22% of AAI
$15,901 to $20,000	$3,498 + 25% of AAI over $15,900
$20,001 to $24,100	$4,523 + 29% of AAI over $20,000
$24,101 to $28,200	$5,712 + 34% of AAI over $24,100
$28,201 to $32,200	$7,106 + 40% of AAI over $28,200
$32,201 or more	$8,706 + 47% of AAI over $32,200

If your family's income (not adjusted) is less than $24,000 per year, your child qualifies for Auto-Zero EFC without looking at assets at all. If your family's income is less than $50,000 per year and you can file a 1040A or 1040EZ tax return, your child qualifies for a Simplified Needs Test that calculates EFC without looking at assets.[113] The Auto-Zero EFC and Simplified Needs Test give you a lower EFC than you would have if you had to report your assets and they can sometimes save you tens of thousands of dollars on educational expenses.

Your Asset Protection Allowance changes based upon the age of the older parent in your household.

[113] https://www.edvisors.com/fafsa/eligibility/simplified-needs-test/

Table A5: Parents' Education Savings and Asset Protection Allowance for EFC Formula A Worksheet (parents only)					
*Age of older parent as of 12/31/2016**	*Allowance if there are two parents***	*Allowance if there is only one parent*	*Age of older parent as of 12/31/2016**	*Allowance if there are two parents***	*Allowance if there is only one parent*
25 or less	$0	$0	46	$17,800	$9,000
26	1,000	500	47	18,300	9,200
27	2,100	1,100	48	18,700	9,400
28	3,100	1,600	49	19,200	9,700
29	4,100	2,100	50	19,700	9,900
30	5,200	2,600	51	20,200	10,100
31	6,200	3,200	52	20,700	10,400
32	7,200	3,700	53	21,300	10,600
33	8,300	4,200	54	21,800	10,900
34	9,300	4,700	55	22,400	11,100
35	10,300	5,300	56	23,000	11,400
36	11,400	5,800	57	23,700	11,700
37	12,400	6,300	58	24,300	12,000
38	13,400	6,800	59	25,000	12,300
39	14,500	7,400	60	25,700	12,600
40	15,500	7,900	61	26,400	12,900
41	15,900	8,100	62	27,200	13,200
42	16,300	8,300	63	27,900	13,600
43	16,600	8,500	64	28,800	13,900
44	17,000	8,600	65 or older	29,600	14,300
45	17,400	8,800			

* Determine the age of the older parent listed in FAFSA/SAR #64 and #68 as of 12/31/2016. If no parent date of birth is provide, use age 45.

** Use the two parent allowance when the Parents' Marital Status listed in FAFSA/SAR #59 is "married or remarried" or "unmarried and both parents are living together."

After the Asset Protection Allowance, your assets will contribute up to 5.64% towards your EFC. It's important to know what counts towards assets and what doesn't. The most noticeable exception is that retirement accounts, such as 401(k)s and IRAs whether roth or traditional, and HSAs do not count towards your assets. 529 Plans do count towards your assets. Small family businesses do not count towards your assets on the FAFSA but do on the CSS Profile. Below is a table showing reportable assets and non-reportable assets for the FAFSA.[114]

Reportable Assets	Non-Reportable Assets
• Cash (even if stuffed in a mattress) • Bank accounts, including checking accounts, savings accounts and CDs • Brokerage accounts • Money market accounts • Investments, such as stocks, bonds, mutual funds, stock options, restricted stock units (RSUs), exchange-traded funds (ETFs), hedge funds, REITs and commodities • Precious metals • UGMAs and UTMAs • College Savings Plans, including 529 plans, prepaid tuition plans and Coverdell Education Savings Accounts • Businesses • Investment farms • Real estate • Trust funds • Emergency funds	• Principal place of residence (family home) • Family farms • Small businesses owned and controlled by the family (less than 100 FTE employees and family members own more than half the business) • Qualified retirement plan accounts, such as 401(k), 403(b), 457, pensions, annuities, traditional IRAs, Roth IRAs, Roth 401(k), SEP, SIMPLE and Keogh plans • Life insurance policies, such as cash value and whole life • Personal possessions, such as cars, boats, computers, software, clothing, jewelry, furniture, television sets, stereo equipment, appliances

When to Contribute to 529 Plans

Because of the downsides of paying income tax on earnings instead of lower capital gains tax and potentially an additional 10% penalty if the funds aren't used for education, 529s are risky. You will find a better return on your money funding retirement accounts more than 529s since in addition to being capital gains tax-free they also are income tax-free or deferred and will not count against your EFC for financial aid. If you are already maxing out your retirement accounts and plan to be earning more than $24,000 per year when your children go to school, it makes sense to fund up to around 188% (47% * 4 years of education) of your adjusted allowable income to a 529 plan. That will be around 0.5% of your adjusted allowable yearly income

[114] https://www.cappex.com/hq/articles-and-advice/financial-aid/fafsa/How-to-Shelter-Assets-on-the-FAFSA

each month over 18 years, 1.2% over 10 years, or 2.7% over 5 years. These are low, safe estimates since you definitely do not want to overfund your 529. If you believe you will be making less than $25,000 per year by the time your kids go to college, such as if you retire early and withdraw less than $25,000 from your retirement accounts, then you should channel that money into a taxable account instead of a 529.

Financial Priorities

1. Automate expense tracking and establish categorized budgets to control and predict your spending.
2. Project your finances to reveal the future impact of your spending and saving.
3. Save one month's income in an easily accessible checking account as a bank account buffer.
4. Sign up for a HSA if a High Deductible Health Plan saves you premiums or your employer contributes to your Health Savings Account. Contribute up to your employer's maximum match for free money in this HSA. If your employer's HSA match percentage is lower than their 401(k) match percentage, max out your 401(k) match before maxing out your HSA match.
5. If your employer matches contributions to your 401(k), contribute up to the maximum match for free money and invest it in low fee global market stock portfolio and domestic bond funds, increasing bond allocation as you approach retirement.
6. Save up to your expected yearly medical expenses in a HSA if you are covered by a High Deductible Health Plan for triple tax-free medical expenses.
7. Monitor and increase your credit score.
8. Pay down credit card debt in order of descending interest rate while rotating balances over 0-interest cards.
9. Earn cashback rewards on your purchases.
10. Subtract your bank account buffer from your desired emergency fund and invest twice that amount for up to four to ten months' expenses in a Roth IRA up to the max (through a Backdoor Roth IRA or Mega Backdoor Roth IRA if necessary) then a taxable investment account for a safe, high-earning emergency fund.

11. Start saving for any short term goals such as a wedding or down payment on a house in a savings account until reaching your goal then match additional savings from income with money from your savings account and invest it in a Roth IRA up to the max (through a Backdoor Roth IRA or Mega Backdoor Roth IRA if necessary and available) then a taxable investment account until it reaches double the amount of your goal. Utilize tax loss harvesting and tax efficient asset placement to minimize your taxable investment account's taxes.
12. Buy your financial independence by saving a target percentage of your gross income minus taxes (minimum 15%) to retire by your desired date and invest it in a tax optimal manner among your HSA, IRAs, 401(k)s, and taxable investment account. Stop using HSA funds to cover medical expenses, leaving HSA funds to compound earnings without tax-drag, and save medical receipts for future tax-free HSA withdrawals.
13. If you want to invest for future pre-retirement spending instead of using all your savings to buy financial independence, invest further savings in a tax efficient manner among your Roth IRA, Roth 401(k), and taxable investment account.
14. **If you are already maxing out your retirement accounts and plan to be earning more than $24,000 per year when your children go to school, it makes sense to fund up to around 188% (47% * 4 years of education) of your adjusted allowable income to a 529 plan. That will be around 0.5% of your adjusted allowable yearly income each month over 18 years, 1.2% over 10 years, or 2.7% over 5 years. If you believe you will be making less than $24,000 per year by the time your kids go to college, such as if you retire early and withdraw less than $24,000 from your retirement accounts, then you should channel that money into a taxable account instead of a 529. Any excess savings after funding your 529 should go towards investing in a taxable investment account or paying down debt.**

Chapter 12 – Paying Down "Good" Debt

After paying down credit card debt you may find your only remaining debt is "good debt." Good debt is any debt with an effective (after tax deductions) interest rate lower than your expected return on stocks; conversely, bad debt is any debt with an effective interest rate greater than or equal to your expected return on stocks. In 2018 your expected return on stocks is around 7.5%. Any bad debt should be paid down as quickly as possible, using the approach we outlined in Chapter 7 – Credit Cards, before investing outside of your HSA and 401(k) matches. Assuming your credit score is good (670+), your car loans, student loans, and mortgages likely all fall under the good debt category.

Paying down your good debt provides a no-risk return equivalent to the debt's interest rate, which is usually higher than bond returns and therefore a better investment than bonds. In Chapter 5 – 401(k)s we discussed calculating your stock allocation vs bond allocation. This allocation split can really be thought of as a "growth allocation" and a "risk-averse allocation." Instead of investing your contributions' risk-averse allocation in bonds, you can use it to pay down good debt by calculating what percentage of your excess investment money—money after paying monthly debt minimums, securing employer matches, and building an emergency fund—should be reserved for debt repayment. However, because the return of debt repayment is greater than investing in bonds, your debt-repayment allocation should be higher than your bond allocation.

Two factors go into calculating your debt-repayment allocation: what percentage of your contributions should be risk-averse (bond allocation) and how the loan's interest rate compares to the expected return on bonds (3%). To take both factors into account, multiply your bond allocation by the loan's effective (after-tax) interest rate divided by the expected return on bonds.

[Percent of excess investment money to reserve for paying debt] = [Bond allocation] * ([Highest effective loan interest rate] / [Expected return on bonds])

For example, if you are 20 years from retirement and your car loan is your highest effective loan interest rate at 6%, you would reserve [10% Bond allocation] * ([6% Effective car loan interest rate] / [3% Expected return on bonds]) = 20% of excess investment money to pay down that car loan faster than your minimum payments. Once you pay off that loan, move on to your next highest effective loan interest rate. This approach will prevent that high interest rate from building your loan balance.

As mentioned in Chapter 7 – Credit Cards, some financial advisors will recommend that you pay down the loan with the lowest balance to give you the psychological win of paying off a particular loan completely, but you will take the net-worth optimized approach of paying down the highest interest rate debt first. The remaining 80% of excess investment money would all be invested into your stock allocation and 0% into bonds. If you already have bonds in your taxable account or Roth IRA, you can consider selling those to help pay down your debt. Don't do this with other tax-advantaged accounts as doing so might incur penalties. Also, don't eat into your emergency funds or funds reserved for short-term goals.

Maintaining Liquidity

One valid argument against paying down good debt is the resulting loss of liquidity. Unlike bonds which you can sell for cash, once you pay down a loan, you can't get that money back. While for mortgages you can open up a Home Equity Line of Credit (HELOC), a bank could freeze your access to taking out money from the HELOC at any point. Therefore, if you have reason to maintain liquidity in addition to your emergency fund, it can sometimes make sense to allocate your non-equity investments to bonds rather than debt. Due to its negative impact on your net worth, this is not recommended for any debts with an effective interest rate more than 1-2% above your expected bond return rate, but if your remaining debts all are close to bond rates, you can consider saving for long-term possibilities such as a predetermined length sabbatical before allocating additional savings to debt.

Financial Priorities

1. Automate expense tracking and establish categorized budgets to control and predict your spending.
2. Project your finances to reveal the future impact of your spending and saving.
3. Save one month's income in an easily accessible checking account as a bank account buffer.
4. Sign up for a HSA if a High Deductible Health Plan saves you premiums or your employer contributes to your Health Savings Account. Contribute up to your employer's maximum match for free money in this HSA. If your employer's HSA match percentage is lower than their 401(k) match percentage, max out your 401(k) match before maxing out your HSA match.
5. If your employer matches contributions to your 401(k), contribute up to the maximum match for free money and invest it in low fee global market stock portfolio and domestic bond funds, increasing bond allocation as you approach retirement.
6. Save up to your expected yearly medical expenses in a HSA if you are covered by a High Deductible Health Plan for triple tax-free medical expenses.
7. Monitor and increase your credit score.
8. Pay down credit card debt in order of descending interest rate while rotating balances over 0-interest cards.
9. Earn cashback rewards on your purchases.
10. Subtract your bank account buffer from your desired emergency fund and invest twice that amount for up to four to ten months' expenses in a Roth IRA up to the max (through a Backdoor Roth IRA or Mega Backdoor Roth IRA if necessary) then a taxable investment account for a safe, high-earning emergency fund.
11. Start saving for any short term goals such as a wedding or down payment on a house in a savings account until reaching your goal then match additional savings from income with money from your savings account and invest it in a Roth IRA up to the max (through a Backdoor Roth IRA or Mega Backdoor Roth IRA if necessary and available) then a taxable investment account until it reaches double the amount of your goal.

Utilize tax loss harvesting and tax efficient asset placement to minimize your taxable investment account's taxes.

12. **Set aside your excess savings—money after paying monthly debt minimums, securing employer matches, and building an emergency fund—and allocate a percentage of it equal to your target bond allocation multiplied by your highest effective interest rate loan divided by the expected return on bonds to pay off your highest effective interest rate loan. If all remaining debts have an effective interest rate no more than 1-2% above effective bond return rates and you have possible long-term needs for liquidity, you can invest in bonds to achieve your liquidity goal before directing further savings to paying down this debt.**
13. Buy your financial independence by saving a target percentage of your gross income minus taxes (minimum 15%) to retire by your desired date and invest it in a tax optimal manner among your HSA, IRAs, 401(k)s, and taxable investment account. Stop using HSA funds to cover medical expenses, leaving HSA funds to compound earnings without tax-drag, and save medical receipts for future tax-free HSA withdrawals.
14. If you want to invest for future pre-retirement spending instead of using all your savings to buy financial independence, invest further savings in a tax efficient manner among your Roth IRA, Roth 401(k), and taxable investment account.
15. If you are already maxing out your retirement accounts and plan to be earning more than $24,000 per year when your children go to school, it makes sense to fund up to around 188% (47% * 4 years of education) of your adjusted allowable income to a 529 plan. That will be around 0.5% of your adjusted allowable yearly income each month over 18 years, 1.2% over 10 years, or 2.7% over 5 years. If you believe you will be making less than $25,000 per year by the time your kids go to college, such as if you retire early and withdraw less than $25,000 from your retirement accounts, then you should channel that money into a taxable account instead of a 529. Any excess savings after funding your 529 should go towards investing in a taxable investment account or paying down debt.

Chapter 13 – Car Loans

Buying A Car

Let's start by bringing to light the most important fact about cars with your finances: they're usually the worst investment one can make. According to CarFax.com, "The minute a person drives a new car off the lot it loses approximately 10 percent of its value. By the end of the first year, that car will lose an additional 10 percent.... On average, a new car will lose 60% of its total value over the first five years of its life."[115] But for many, a car is necessary to get to and from work in a comfortable and timely fashion. Because of this, the most financially effective means of car buying is to buy a used, fuel efficient, reliable, cheap car.

Cars are very personal for many people and you may be determined to buy a particular, pricier car. By all means if such a car genuinely brings you sustained enjoyment, you should feel free to do so; just know that such cars often cost tens of thousands of dollars that can't be invested, they depreciate in value, and come with insurance and fuel costs that can amount to several thousands of dollars per year. No matter what car you buy, be sure to negotiate the costs and use a reputable cost estimator such as Kelley Blue Book at kbb.com, True Car at TrueCar.com, or Cars Direct at CarsDirect.com to come to the negotiation offering the lowest quote among those sites.

If you are buying from a dealer, any discounts or incentives you've researched should be applied *after* you've negotiated the sale price. Additionally, negotiate the sale price separately from the trade in value of your car if you want to sell your car to the dealer; however, I recommend selling your car separately using a site like Craig's List because you will usually get more money for your car this way. Also, keep in mind that financing is also a negotiation and unless you are given a deal on low financing (0-4% interest rate) you are often better getting financing yourself away from a dealership. The dealer will likely try to sell you a bunch of

---

[115] https://www.carfax.com/blog/car-depreciation/

extras after agreeing on the car purchase and you almost always are wise to reject all of them.

If you buy directly from a car owner, be sure to have the car inspected before the purchase by an independent mechanic. These inspections typically cost between $100 and $200 and are well worth avoiding buying a car with problems.

Leasing vs Owning

Unless you believe you'll want a different car within the next three years, it doesn't make sense to lease a car. While buying a car does have higher monthly payments, once the loan is paid off you have an asset—your car—to either continue driving without payment or to sell. If you will need a different car in three years, leasing a car has the benefit of lower monthly payments and given the car will be depreciating a lot over the next three years, you probably wouldn't be able to recuperate the additional amount you paid in monthly payments by selling the car after three years. Modern cars often have life spans of around 200,000 miles which for many will last them more than 10 years. For most people, buying a car and holding it for as long as possible is the smartest move financially.

Consumer Reports walked through a typical example of financing a car over six years vs leasing it for six years. In their example, buying saved almost 10% of the cost of leasing.[116]

	6-Year Loan	**2 Back-to-Back 3-Year Leases**
Monthly Payment	$416.00	$287.00
Down Payment	$2,000	-
Cash Due at Signing	-	$2,000
Interest Rate	2.9%	0.024% (Money Factor .00001)[117]
Total Paid After 3 Years	$16,976	$12,332
Residual Value	-	$16,994

---

[116] https://www.consumerreports.org/buying-a-car/leasing-vs-buying-a-new-car/
[117] https://www.investopedia.com/terms/m/money-factor.asp

After 3 Years		
Total Paid After 6 Years	$31,952	$24,664 (two leases back to back, including two payments of $2,000 at signing)
Resale Value at Age 6	$9,675	You don't have a car to sell
Final Cost	$22,277	$24,664
Savings	**9.7%**	

Financing A Car

Depending on your credit, car loan interest rates can range from 2% - 15%.[118] Oftentimes the lowest rates come from your local credit union. Credit unions operate similar to banks except that they are not-for-profit financial cooperatives whose earnings are paid back to members in the form of higher savings rates or lower loan rates. You can compare your local credit unions' rates against reputable and cheap online financiers such as myautoloan.com and lightstream.com. It's beneficial to keep your car loan as long as you anticipate you'll be paying down a higher interest loan. If you have higher interest loans that you anticipate won't be paid off for around half a decade, consider taking out a car loan of 5-7 years; if you don't have higher interest loans, it makes sense to consider a 2-3 year loan or better yet paying for the car in cash. Car loans do not come with any tax deductions, so the stated interest rate is also the effective interest rate.

Financial Priorities

1. Automate expense tracking and establish categorized budgets to control and predict your spending.
2. Project your finances to reveal the future impact of your spending and saving.
3. Save one month's income in an easily accessible checking account as a bank account buffer.
4. Sign up for a HSA if a High Deductible Health Plan saves you premiums or your employer contributes to your Health Savings Account. Contribute

[118] https://www.gobankingrates.com/loans/credit-score-determines-auto-loan-apr/

up to your employer's maximum match for free money in this HSA. If your employer's HSA match percentage is lower than their 401(k) match percentage, max out your 401(k) match before maxing out your HSA match.

5. If your employer matches contributions to your 401(k), contribute up to the maximum match for free money and invest it in low fee global market stock portfolio and domestic bond funds, increasing bond allocation as you approach retirement.
6. Save up to your expected yearly medical expenses in a HSA if you are covered by a High Deductible Health Plan for triple tax-free medical expenses.
7. Monitor and increase your credit score.
8. Pay down credit card debt in order of descending interest rate while rotating balances over 0-interest cards.
9. Earn cashback rewards on your purchases.
10. Subtract your bank account buffer from your desired emergency fund and invest twice that amount for up to four to ten months' expenses in a Roth IRA up to the max (through a Backdoor Roth IRA or Mega Backdoor Roth IRA if necessary) then a taxable investment account for a safe, high-earning emergency fund.
11. Start saving for any short term goals such as a wedding or down payment on a house in a savings account until reaching your goal then match additional savings from income with money from your savings account and invest it in a Roth IRA up to the max (through a Backdoor Roth IRA or Mega Backdoor Roth IRA if necessary and available) then a taxable investment account until it reaches double the amount of your goal. Utilize tax loss harvesting and tax efficient asset placement to minimize your taxable investment account's taxes.
12. Set aside your excess savings—money after paying monthly debt minimums, securing employer matches, and building an emergency fund—and allocate a percentage of it equal to your target non-equity allocation multiplied by your highest effective interest rate loan divided by the expected return on bonds to pay off your highest effective interest rate loan. If all remaining debts have an effective interest rate no more than 1% above effective bond return rates and you have possible long-term needs for liquidity, you can invest in bonds to achieve

your liquidity goal before directing further savings to paying down this debt.

a. **Spend less on your car by buying instead of leasing unless you expect you'll want another new car within 3 years. If you expect to have higher interest debt for the foreseeable future, finance over 5-7 years; otherwise, finance over 2-3 years.**

13. Buy your financial independence by saving a target percentage of your gross income minus taxes (minimum 15%) to retire by your desired date and invest it in a tax optimal manner among your HSA, IRAs, 401(k)s, and taxable investment account. Stop using HSA funds to cover medical expenses, leaving HSA funds to compound earnings without tax-drag, and save medical receipts for future tax-free HSA withdrawals.
14. If you want to invest for future pre-retirement spending instead of using all your savings to buy financial independence, invest further savings in a tax efficient manner among your Roth IRA, Roth 401(k), and taxable investment account.
15. If you are already maxing out your retirement accounts and plan to be earning more than $24,000 per year when your children go to school, it makes sense to fund up to around 188% (47% * 4 years of education) of your adjusted allowable income to a 529 plan. That will be around 0.5% of your adjusted allowable yearly income each month over 18 years, 1.2% over 10 years, or 2.7% over 5 years. If you believe you will be making less than $25,000 per year by the time your kids go to college, such as if you retire early and withdraw less than $25,000 from your retirement accounts, then you should channel that money into a taxable account instead of a 529. Any excess savings after funding your 529 should go towards investing in a taxable investment account or paying down debt.

Chapter 14 – Student Loans

Student loan interest rates typically range between 3%-13%. As long as your income isn't above $80,000 for single filers or $165,000 for married filing jointly filers, student loan interest can be deducted off your taxes so the effective student loan interest rate that is only 72 - 85% of the actual rate.[119]

Types of Student Loans

Student loans can come from three main sources: the Federal Direct Student Loan Program (FDSLP) who offers "direct loans," the Federal Family Education Loan Program who offers "FFEL loans," and private companies who offer "private loans." Direct loans are funded by the U.S. Treasury directly whereas FFEL loans are funded by banks or credit unions, but the policies of both types of loans are set by congress. While direct loans and FFEL are similar, some direct loans have slightly favorable interest rates and are sometimes easier to qualify for, but the availability of each program depends on the school you attend.[120]

- Stafford Loans
  - Stafford loans are loans granted directly to the student. Stafford loans come in two forms: subsidized or unsubsidized. If your loan is subsidized, you won't be responsible for interest accruing while attending school, but these loans are only available to lower income families typically making $50,000 or less per year. Subsidized loans are only available to undergraduate students and come with a maximum annual amount that depends on your class. Unsubsidized loans will charge interest while in school, but you aren't required to make payments until you are done with school. All Stafford loans come with an annual maximum that depends on whether the student is dependent or independent according to the Free Application for

[119] https://www.irs.gov/publications/p970/ch04.html
[120] http://www.finaid.org/loans/dl-vs-ffel.phtml

Federal Student Aid (FAFSA) form.[121] If your parents are ineligible for PLUS loans, you are considered an independent.[122]

Grade Level	Dependent Students	Independent Students
Freshman: 0 – 29 credit hours	$5,500 (no more than $3,500 subsidized)	$9,500 (no more than $3,500 subsidized)
Sophomore: 30 – 59 credit hours	$6,500 (no more than $4,500 subsidized)	$10,500 (no more than $4,500 subsidized)
Junior/Senior: 60+ credit hours	$7,500 (no more than $5,500 subsidized)	$12,500 (no more than $5,500 subsidized)
Graduate Students	N/A	$20,500 (Graduate students are not eligible to receive subsidized loans)
PhD Candidates in Human Services Psychology, Clinical Psychology Concentration ONLY	N/A	$33,000 (Graduate students are not eligible to receive subsidized loans)

- Perkins Loans
    - Perkins loans are granted to need-based college students but are no longer offered as of September 30, 2017. These loans were more desirable than Stafford loans because they had a fixed interest rate of 5% and were subsidized such that you wouldn't be charged interest while attending school. They also had a 9-month grace period after ending school before payments began and came with additional loan forgiveness provisions.
- PLUS Loans
    - PLUS loans are offered by the government to parents of dependent undergraduate students or graduate students. There are no annual maximums to these loans and they can be used to cover any education costs not covered by other financial aid.
- Consolidation Loans

[121] https://studentaid.ed.gov/sa/fafsa/filling-out/dependency
[122] http://financialaid.umbc.edu/types-of-aid/federal-loans/stafford-limits/

- Any of the above loans that have been consolidated into a single loan.
- Private Loans
  - Similar to personal loans, private loans depend on your credit history, are not subsidized, and deferment and forbearance options are limited. But these loans can cover your expenses if federal loans don't cover your needs.[123]

Early Student Loan Forgiveness

- Public Service Loan Forgiveness
  - Qualifying public employees including firefighters, teachers, military personnel, teachers, and nurses working fulltime for a nonprofit or government entity for at least 10 years can have their federal loans forgiven.
- Teacher Loan Forgiveness
  - Teachers in K-12 schools working full-time for five consecutive years can have up to $17,500 in Stafford or Perkins loans forgiven. While you can participate in both the Teacher Loan Forgiveness and Public Service Loan Forgiveness programs, you cannot serve time in both of them simultaneously. If you have a loan balance expected to be around $17,500 within 5 years, the Student Loan Forgiveness program will benefit you and after that you can still apply for the Public Service Loan Forgiveness program. If your loan balance is much higher and you only anticipate teaching for about 10 years, you may want to apply for the Public Service Loan Forgiveness program instead of the Teach Loan Forgiveness program such that all your student loans are forgiven after 10 years.[124]
- Perkins Loan Cancellation
  - Qualifying public employees working in qualifying public service positions may have up to 100%,[125]typically a percentage of loans for each year served, of their Perkins loans cancelled.[126]

---

[123]https://www.debt.org/students/types-of-loans/
[124]https://www.nerdwallet.com/blog/loans/student-loans/student-loan-forgiveness/
[125]https://ifap.ed.gov/fsahandbook/attachments/0910FSAHbkVol6Ch5Oct2.pdf
[126]https://studentaid.ed.gov/sa/repay-loans/forgiveness-cancellation/charts#perkins-loan-cancellation

Student Loan Repayment Plans

Repayment plans decide your monthly payments, length of repayment, and sometimes come with benefits. We will review the details of the federal loan repayment plans and afterwards we'll review which plans are best for particular circumstances.

- Regular Repayment Plans
  - Standard Repayment Plan
    - Payments
      - Payments are fixed over 10 to 30 years depending on the outstanding balance of the loan.
  - Graduated Repayment Plan
    - Payments
      - Payments start lower, then slowly increase every couple of years for the same period as the Standard Repayment Plan.
  - Extended Repayment Plan
    - Payments
      - Payments may be fixed or graduated but all balances have up to 25 years to repay the loan.
    - Qualifying
      - To qualify you must have at least $30,000 in loans.
    - Disadvantage
      - Not eligible for early loan forgiveness.[127]
- Income Driven Repayment Plans
  - Pay As You Earn Repayment Plan (PAYE)
    - Qualifying
      - To qualify, you must be required to pay less than the Standard Repayment Plan.
      - You must also be a new borrower as of Oct. 1, 2007, and must have received a disbursement of a Direct Loan on or after Oct. 1, 2011.[128]
    - Payments

---

[127] http://www.equaljusticeworks.org/ed-debt/employers/public-service-loan-forgiveness/qualifying-payments

[128] https://studentaid.ed.gov/sa/repay-loans/understand/plans/income-driven#ibr-pay-as-you-earn

- Minimum payments are capped at 10% of your (and your spouses' only if you file taxes jointly) discretionary income (income in excess of 150% of the family poverty level). If your income increases such that you'd owe more than the standard repayment plan, you will only owe as much as the standard repayment plan.[129]

- Benefits
    - Accrued interest that capitalizes (interest added to your principal, instead of a separate "interest balance," such that it starts being charged interest) on the loan cannot grow greater than 10% of the balance of your loans at the time you entered the repayment plan. New interest starts capitalizing once your payments would be more than the standard repayment plan.
    - The remaining balance after 20 years is forgiven. The amount forgiven is taxed as income.

- Revised Pay As You Earn Repayment Plan (REPAYE)
    - Payments
        - This plan was introduced to allow more people to qualify for the plan as it doesn't require payments to be less than the Standard Repayment Plan. Like the PAYE Repayment Plan, minimum payments are capped at 10% of your discretionary income (but unlike the PAYE Plan it includes your spouses' income regardless of how you file taxes). However, the plan has no cap so you can end up paying more per month than the Standard Repayment Plan if your income increases.
    - Benefits
        - Includes a subsidy such that if your monthly payments don't cover the monthly accrued interest on your loans, the government will pay half that monthly accrued interest.
        - Interest never capitalizes unless you leave the REPAYE plan.[130]
        - The remaining balance after 20 years is forgiven, 25 years if any loans under the plan were for graduate or professional study. The amount forgiven is taxed as income.

---

[129] https://studentloansherpa.com/discretionary-income-calculation/

[130] http://www.benwhite.com/finance/paye-vs-repaye-interest-capitalization-cap-better-than-interest-subsidy/

- Income-Based Repayment Plan (IBR)
  - Qualifying
    - To qualify, you must be required to pay less than the Standard Repayment Plan.
  - Payments
    - Minimum payments are capped at 10% of your discretionary income if you're a new borrower after July 1st 2014 or 15% of your discretionary income if not. If your income increases such that you'd owe more than the standard repayment plan, you will only owe as much as the standard repayment plan.
  - Benefits
    - The remaining balance after 20 years is forgiven if you're a borrower on or after July 1st, 2014; otherwise, 25 years. The amount forgiven is taxed as income.
- Income-Contingent Repayment Plan (ICR)
  - Payments
    - Minimum payments are capped at the lesser of 20% of your discretionary income or what you pay on a 12-year fixed payment plan.
  - Benefits
    - The remaining balance after 25 years is forgiven.
- Income-Sensitive Repayment Plan
  - Qualifying
    - Only FFEL loans are eligible.
  - Payments
    - You pick your monthly minimum payment of 4-25% of your gross monthly income, but the payment must be at least enough to cover any accrued interest. This plan can be chosen for up to five years and does not increase the term of the loan, meaning that the remaining five years have their payments make up the difference.[131]

When pursuing an early student loan forgiveness or cancellation plan (loans forgiven in 10 or less years), your goal is to keep minimum payments as cheap as possible until your loans are forgiven. You can calculate your

[131] https://studentaid.ed.gov/sa/repay-loans/understand/plans

payments using the Federal Student Aid's repayment calculator.[132] Unless a spouse earns significant income with a low student loan balance, the cheapest plan is REPAYE because of its accrued interest subsidy, but as your income rises making you pay more than the Standard Repayment Plan, you may wish you had chosen PAYE or IBR which caps payments at those of the Standard Repayment Plan. The solution to this is to start under REPAYE then switch to PAYE, preferably, or IBR, secondly, before your income increases such that you become ineligible. Once you switch out of REPAYE your interest will capitalize, but it will be forgiven anyways.[133] If a spouse earns enough income with a low student loan balance, REPAYE stops being a good deal since it considers your household income regardless of how you file taxes and you should just apply for PAYE or IBR from the beginning and file taxes separately. You will need to determine if the REPAYE subsidy outweighs any tax hit from filing taxes separately.

If you aren't pursuing early student loan forgiveness, your goal is to keep minimum payments as low as possible such that you have the option to pay off higher interest debt or invest and only pay down additional student loan debt when it becomes your priority. Your approach would be the same as with student loan forgiveness, start in REPAYE if beneficial then switch to PAYE or IBR shortly before becoming ineligible or having a spouse's income make those plans a better deal. If you are still paying off graduate or professional loans under REPAYE for a forgiveness period of 25 years, you can switch over to PAYE shortly before the 20 year point such that your loan is forgiven after 20 years. The ability to switch between plans and have previous payments made on one plan count towards the forgiveness of another plan is supported by the Federal Student Aid documentation: "If you were previously in repayment under one income-driven repayment plan and later switched to a different income-driven repayment plan, payments you made under both plans will generally count toward the required years of qualifying monthly payments for the new plan."

If you make too much for a subsidy from REPAYE, it's likely the Extended Repayment Plan will be best if you have more than $30,000 in loans, if not, then the Graduated Repayment Plan or Income-Contingent Repayment Plan

[132] https://studentloans.gov/myDirectLoan/mobile/repayment/repaymentEstimator.action
[133] http://www.benwhite.com/finance/yes-you-can-switch-back-from-repaye-to-ibr-or-paye/

depending on which provides lower payments based on income. I advise against the Income-Sensitive Repayment Plan unless necessary to afford your FFEL loans because while it can reduce your payment significantly, it comes at the cost of greatly increasing your minimum payment—potentially to an unaffordable level—in the not-too-distant future. Note that these non-early forgiveness plans tend to be so long such that you will benefit more from paying them down early instead of continuing to accrue interest and having some forgiven.

Student Loan Consolidation and Refinancing

One option you may have available is to consolidate your student loans into one single loan. Sometimes this is necessary to have all your loans qualify for a desired payment plan, in which case it almost always makes sense to consolidate. The resulting loan typically has an interest rate that's a weighted average of your other loans. Unless you need to consolidate for a repayment plan, consolidating is generally not a good idea because it eliminates your ability to pay down your higher interest student loans first. The benefit of consolidation is that your minimum monthly payment typically decreases allowing you to allocate that money elsewhere. Lower minimum payments at the expense of effectively higher interest is usually a bad deal with the exception of if you are pursuing early student loan forgiveness, in which case it makes sense.

An option that sometimes can be a good idea is refinancing your student loans with a reputable private company such as SoFi, Social Finance, Inc. at www.sofi.com.[134] SoFi can sometimes refinance your student loans at a rate that is lower than the weighted average of your other loans. If you apply for such a refinance, and their rate is lower than the weighted average of your student loans, you should refinance unless you are pursuing early loan forgiveness since private companies are not eligible for such forgiveness. To calculate the weighted average of your student loans, sum up the product of the student loan interest rate and the percentage of the balance of that loan for all your loans like so:

---

[134] https://studentloanhero.com/5-banks-to-refinance-your-student-loans-0081/

([Interest rate loan 1] * ([Balance loan 1] / [Balance all loans])) + ([Interest rate loan 2] * ([Balance loan 2] / [Balance all loans])) + ... + ([Interest rate loan n] * ([Balance loan n] / [Balance all loans]))

Financial Priorities

1. Automate expense tracking and establish categorized budgets to control and predict your spending.
2. Project your finances to reveal the future impact of your spending and saving.
3. Save one month's income in an easily accessible checking account as a bank account buffer.
4. Sign up for a HSA if a High Deductible Health Plan saves you premiums or your employer contributes to your Health Savings Account. Contribute up to your employer's maximum match for free money in this HSA. If your employer's HSA match percentage is lower than their 401(k) match percentage, max out your 401(k) match before maxing out your HSA match.
5. If your employer matches contributions to your 401(k), contribute up to the maximum match for free money and invest it in low fee global market stock portfolio and domestic bond funds, increasing bond allocation as you approach retirement.
6. Save up to your expected yearly medical expenses in a HSA if you are covered by a High Deductible Health Plan for triple tax-free medical expenses.
7. Monitor and increase your credit score.
8. Pay down credit card debt in order of descending interest rate while rotating balances over 0-interest cards.
9. Earn cashback rewards on your purchases.
10. Subtract your bank account buffer from your desired emergency fund and invest twice that amount for up to four to ten months' expenses in a Roth IRA up to the max (through a Backdoor Roth IRA or Mega Backdoor Roth IRA if necessary) then a taxable investment account for a safe, high-earning emergency fund.
11. Start saving for any short term goals such as a wedding or down payment on a house in a savings account until reaching your goal then match additional savings from income with money from your savings account

and invest it in a Roth IRA up to the max (through a Backdoor Roth IRA or Mega Backdoor Roth IRA if necessary and available) then a taxable investment account until it reaches double the amount of your goal. Utilize tax loss harvesting and tax efficient asset placement to minimize your taxable investment account's taxes.

12. Set aside your excess savings—money after paying monthly debt minimums, securing employer matches, and building an emergency fund—and allocate a percentage of it equal to your target non-equity allocation multiplied by your highest effective interest rate loan divided by the expected return on bonds to pay off your highest effective interest rate loan. If all remaining debts have an effective interest rate no more than 1% above effective bond return rates and you have possible long-term needs for liquidity, you can invest in bonds to achieve your liquidity goal before directing further savings to paying down this debt.
    a. **Spend less on your car by buying instead of leasing unless you expect you'll want another new car within 3 years. If you expect to have higher interest debt for the foreseeable future, finance over 5-7 years; otherwise, finance over 2-3 years.**
    b. **Apply for the lowest monthly payment student loan repayment plan for which you are eligible and early student loan forgiveness if eligible. Refinance with a private company if your weighted average interest rate would be lower than your federal loan rate unless you are pursuing early student loan forgiveness.**
13. Buy your financial independence by saving a target percentage of your gross income minus taxes (minimum 15%) to retire by your desired date and invest it in a tax optimal manner among your HSA, IRAs, 401(k)s, and taxable investment account. Stop using HSA funds to cover medical expenses, leaving HSA funds to compound earnings without tax-drag, and save medical receipts for future tax-free HSA withdrawals.
14. If you want to invest for future pre-retirement spending instead of using all your savings to buy financial independence, invest further savings in a tax efficient manner among your Roth IRA, Roth 401(k), and taxable investment account.
15. If you are already maxing out your retirement accounts and plan to be earning more than $24,000 per year when your children go to school, it makes sense to fund up to around 188% (47% * 4 years of education) of

your adjusted allowable income to a 529 plan. That will be around 0.5% of your adjusted allowable yearly income each month over 18 years, 1.2% over 10 years, or 2.7% over 5 years. If you believe you will be making less than $25,000 per year by the time your kids go to college, such as if you retire early and withdraw less than $25,000 from your retirement accounts, then you should channel that money into a taxable account instead of a 529. Any excess savings after funding your 529 should go towards investing in a taxable investment account or paying down debt.

Chapter 15 – Mortgages

Everyone needs a place to live. This usually takes the form of renting a property or financing homeownership with a mortgage. Mortgages allow you to exchange monthly payments for equity in a property whereas renting allows you to exchange monthly payments for the right to live in a property for that month. For many, homeownership, like car ownership, is the right long-term financial decision as you get an asset in exchange for your money. However, mortgages come with front-loaded mortgage interest, closing costs, and potentially rehab costs. To ensure the mortgage company makes a reasonable return before you sell the house and pay off the mortgage, mortgage amortization schedules are setup such that for the first few years very little of your minimum monthly payments is applied towards paying down the principal of your mortgage and the majority goes towards mortgage interest.[135] This causes you to gain very little equity in your home to make up for the costs of buying and owning a home. However, after a few years, more and more of your mortgage payment is applied towards paying down principal, making the finances of rent-vs-buy come down to how long you'll keep the house.

The rent-vs-buy breakeven point depends on many factors but the rule of thumb is that it makes financial sense to buy a home if you plan on keeping it for at least five years. If you feel confident you'll be settled in an area for at least five years and you've already built up an adequate emergency fund, you should strongly consider saving up for a home down payment. In many rural areas, the breakeven point shortens to as low as about two years and in many urban areas, the breakeven point lengthens to as high as about ten years. You can use the "price to rent ratio" to estimate whether your area is closer to a two-year or ten-year breakeven point.[136]

Price to Rent Ratio = Average sales price/(Average Rental Price * 12)

- Price to rent ratio of 1 to 15 = typically falls in the five year or less breakeven point[137]

---

[135] http://moneyning.com/housing/the-five-year-rule-for-buying-a-house/
[136] https://20somethingfinance.com/price-to-rent-ratio/
[137] https://rentberry.com/blog/lowest-price-to-rent-us

- Price to rent ratio of 16 to 20 = typically falls in the five to seven year breakeven point
- Price to rent ratio of 21 or more = typically falls in the seven to ten+ year breakeven point[138]

The most precise way to determine whether to rent or buy is via a rent vs buy calculator such as the one provided by the New York Times.[139]

What makes buying a home a good investment is not having to shell out money for rent in exchange for no equity. Otherwise, homeownership is more of a liability than an asset. While the price of new homes increased on average by 5.4% annually from 1963 to 2008, the increase doesn't look as impressive after accounting for the increase in new home size and inflation. From 1950 to 2004, the average new home size increased from 983 square feet to 2,394 square feet. When accounting for this increase in size, the price per new home square foot only increased on average by 4.2% annually from 1963 to 2008. This increase doesn't even keep up with the 4.4% annual inflation over the same period.[140] Furthermore, on top of the mortgage interest and closing costs already mentioned, homeownership comes with property taxes and maintenance costs that typically scale with the size of the home. This means that from a financial standpoint, you should only buy as much house as you believe is necessary for your family to grow into.

Types of Mortgages

Fixed Rate vs. Adjustable Rate

Fixed rate mortgages maintain a constant interest rate throughout the entire length of the mortgage such that your monthly payments never change. Adjustable rate mortgages (ARMs) start with a fixed rate usually for five, seven, or ten years (5/1, 7/1, and 10/1 ARMs respectively) but after their initial fixed rate, they can change each year based on movements in an interest rate such as the rate for Treasury securities or the Cost of Funds

[138] https://smartasset.com/mortgage/price-to-rent-ratio-in-us-cities
[139] https://www.nytimes.com/interactive/2014/upshot/buy-rent-calculator.html
[140] https://michaelbluejay.com/house/appreciation.html

Index.[141] Adjustable rate mortgages often hold a lower initial interest rate but come with the potential of increasing over time.

Due to the certainty of fixed rate mortgages and because in 2018 mortgage interest rates are near all-time lows, most people should opt for a fixed rate mortgage. If mortgage rates go down over time, you still have the option of refinancing to take advantage of the lower rates. Adjustable rate mortgages make sense for those who are confident they will be staying in their homes for less than ten years because they come with slightly lower monthly payments than their fixed rate counterparts.

Conventional vs Government-Insured Loans

Conventional Loans

Conventional loans are the most common type of home loan. They require at least 5% of the value of the home towards a down payment; however, if you pay less than 20% down, you are required to pay Private Mortgage Insurance (PMI) to compensate the mortgage company for their risk in lending you such a large percentage of the value of the home. This PMI typically costs the following:

Loan-to-Value	30-year fixed	15-year fixed	Monthly payment
90.01% to 95%	PMI 0.62% of loan	PMI 0.57% of loan	$52/$48 per $100,000 borrowed
85.01% to 90%	PMI 0.44% of loan	PMI 0.39% of loan	$37/$33 per $100,000 borrowed
85% and under	PMI 0.27% of loan	PMI 0.22% of loan	$23/$18 per $100,000 borrowed

Once your loan-to-value ratio falls to 80% or lower, you can call your mortgage company requesting them to drop the PMI and they often will. The federal Homeowners Protection Act requires lenders to automatically cancel PMI once your loan-to-value ratio falls to 78% or lower.[142]

[141] http://www.freddiemac.com/research/datasets/cofi.html
[142] http://www.interest.com/mortgage/news/what-you-need-to-know-about-private-mortgage-insurance/

FHA Loans

The federal Department of Housing and Urban Development (HUD) manages a program called the Federal Housing Administration (FHA) mortgage insurance program. This program is designed to help people become homeowners with the following benefits:

- Smaller down payment
  - o You can pay as little as 3.5% of the value of the purchase towards a down payment.
- Easier approval than conventional loans
  - o Credit scores can be as low as 500 whereas conventional loans often require scores of at least 700.[143]
  - o Debt-to-income ratio, calculated as all monthly debt payments (including mortgage) divided by all monthly income, is capped at 56.9% whereas for conventional loans banks often look for 36% or less.[144]
  - o More forgiving of previous bankruptcy or foreclosure.[145]

However, FHA loans come with the following drawbacks:

- You need to pay an up-front mortgage insurance premium (MIP) that is 1.75% the base loan amount, but this can be rolled into your monthly payments.
- You need to pay an ongoing annual mortgage insurance premium (MIP) with the following rates[146]:

Base Loan Amount	Loan-to-Value (LTV)	Annual MIP
≤ $625,500	≤ 95%	0.80% of mortgage
≤ $625,500	> 95%	0.85% of mortgage
>$625,500	≤ 95%	1.00% of mortgage
> $625,500	> 95%	1.05% of mortgage

---

[143] http://www.homebuyinginstitute.com/mortgagetypes_article6.php
[144] http://www.mortgagecalculator.org/calcs/debt-ratio.php
[145] https://gustancho.com/2017-fha-debt-to-income-ratio-requirements
[146] https://www.fha.com/fha_requirements_mortgage_insurance

For the following periods of time:

Term	LTV%	Previous	New
≤ 15 years	≤ 78%	no annual MIP	11 years
≤ 15 years	78.01% to 90%	cancelled at 78% LTV	11 years
≤ 15 years	> 90%	loan term	loan term
> 15 years	≤ 78%	5 years	11 years
> 15 years	78.01% to 90%	cancelled at 78% LTV and 5 years	11 years
> 15 years	> 90%	cancelled at 78% LTV and 5 years	loan term

VA Loans

The Department of Veterans Affairs (VA) offers a great loan program to military service members and their families. According to the Department of Veterans Affairs, the "VA guarantees a portion of the loan, enabling the lender to provide you with more favorable terms." This loan comes with 100% financing with no private mortgage insurance and tends to be easier to qualify for with lower interest rates than conventional loans. You are eligible for this loan if you meet any one of the following criteria[147]:

- You are a veteran who served 181 days during peacetime (active duty).
- You are a veteran who served 90 days during war time (active duty).
- You served at least 6 years in the National Guard or Reserves.

[147] http://www.homebuyinginstitute.com/news/va-requirements-few-changes-513/

- You are currently on active duty and have served at least 90 continuous days.
- You were discharged from the military due to hardship.
- You are the un-remarried spouse of a veteran who died while in service or from a "service connected disability."

As a drawback, VA loans come with an upfront fee called a VA funding fee. The funding fee typically makes it advantageous put in a down payment of 5% if you can afford to. You could put in a down payment of 10% or 20% to lower or avoid the VA funding fee; however, if you have a high target stock allocation, it makes sense to accept the low funding fee and roll it into the loan leaving the funds liquid to contribute to an emergency fund or invest for a greater return than the funding fee over the course of the next several years.[148]

Regular Military Personnel		
Down Payment	**Funding Fee (1st Use)**	**Funding Fee (Subsequent Use)**
None	2.15 percent	3.3 percent
5-10 percent	1.5 percent	1.5 percent
10 percent and up	1.25 percent	1.25 percent

Reserve & National Guard Personnel

[148] https://www.veteransunited.com/valoans/va-funding-fee-explains-the-fee-who-pays-what-and-why/

Down Payment	Funding Fee (1st Use)	Funding Fee (Subsequent Use)
None	2.4 percent	3.3 percent
5-10 percent	1.75 percent	1.75 percent
10 percent and up	1.5 percent	1.5 percent

USDA / RHS Loans

The United States Department of Agriculture (USDA) offers a loan program for rural borrowers who meet certain income requirements. The program is managed by the Rural Housing Service (RHS), which is part of the Department of Agriculture. This type of mortgage loan is offered to "rural residents who have a steady, low or modest income, and yet are unable to obtain adequate housing through conventional financing." Income must be no higher than 115% of the adjusted area median income (AMI).[149] The loan is similar to VA Loans in that the government guarantees a portion of the loan, enabling the lender to provide you with more favorable terms such as lower interest rates and 0% down. USDA loans come with a 1% upfront USDA Guarantee fee that can be rolled into the mortgage like the VA funding fee and it has a 0.35% annual mortgage insurance fee for the life of the loan.

Loan Duration

The most common home loans are 30-year and 15-year mortgages. Effective mortgage interest rates are typically close to or lower than the returns you will receive investing in bonds, making it another form of good debt. Experts often call fixed rate mortgages a "hedge against inflation." That's because fixed rate mortgages lock in their rate for a lengthy period of time

[149] http://www.homebuyinginstitute.com/mortgagetypes.php

regardless of inflation while other assets such as stocks often grow with inflation as companies can generally pass rising costs on to consumers.[150]

Although 15-year mortgages come with slightly lower interest rates, they also come with higher minimum monthly payments. Instead of using your hard earned money to pay off a relatively low interest rate mortgage, it's often better to pay off higher interest debt or invest that money in a higher yielding portfolio of stocks and bonds, especially since interest rates are near a historical low and are likely to rise with inflation in the future. Furthermore, 30-year loans offer the safety of smaller minimum payments in case you run into financial troubles. If you decide you want to pay off your mortgage faster, you still have the option of increasing your monthly payments. For these reasons, longer term loans such as 30-year loans usually make more financial sense unless your planned mortgage payment according to your percent of excess savings to apply to debt in excess of a 30 year mortgage payment would be greater than or equal to a 15-year mortgage payment. Also, mortgage interest can be tax deductible and so you might get more of an income tax break with a 30-year mortgage. We'll cover mortgage tax deductibility in Chapter 19 – Taxes.

Finding a Loan

If you qualify, a VA loan is your best option followed by a USDA loan. If you can afford to pay 20% down on your loan, a conventional mortgage is your next best option. Otherwise, if you can find a lender offering you a down payment you can afford (such as 10% or even 5% down) that is your next best option. If you are having trouble qualifying for a loan, then you may need to opt for the more expensive FHA loan.

Your choice of lender should almost always come down to who offers you the lowest interest rate with an affordable down payment. It often pays to shop around for rates on sites such as lendingtree.com.[151] One of the lowest rate lenders around with great service is American Internet Mortgage at aimloan.com.[152] American Internet Mortgage saves you money by working

[150] https://www.kitces.com/blog/why-a-mortgage-is-not-actually-an-inflation-hedge-itself-but-can-provide-access-to-investments-that-are/
[151] https://www.lendingtree.com/
[152] https://www.aimloan.com/

directly with you over email and phone and they make the process quite easy. They even guarantee their closing costs, which is often unknown until a few days before closing with other lenders. They also have a price match guarantee if you are able to find a lower rate with another vendor.

American Internet Mortgage also has a rate tracking feature where you can sign up to have them contact you if mortgage rates drop to your target to refinance. Refinancing is the process of taking out a new loan with potentially a different lender and having that new loan pay off your old loan. The reason for refinancing is usually to get a lower interest rate, but keep in mind refinancing might come with closing costs. If rates fall 0.5% or more from your current rate, you should compare the reduced payment for the length of time you expect to keep the house and if the savings are greater than your closing costs, consider refinancing. When refinancing, be sure to implement a rate lock which locks your rate for a period of between 15 and 60 days so that it doesn't increase with interest rate changes before closing.

Titles

A title outlines the ownership rights of a property. When you take out a mortgage, you will need to choose how you will take title. The way you choose your title becomes important when you pass away. Under some titles, the property is subject to probate. Probate is the court-supervised process of distributing a person's assets after death. Probate can take months and even years to settle and can cost up to around 10% the value of the property.[153] Picking the right title can help your heirs avoid probate saving them significant time and money when inheriting your property. The titles available for your property depend on the state in which the property resides.

Sole Ownership

The simplest way to take title is sole ownership. If you are married and you take title as sole ownership, your spouse is typically required to sign a

[153] https://www.legalzoom.com/articles/pros-and-cons-of-probate

quitclaim deed giving up ownership interest in the property. When the sole owner passes away, the property enters probate.

Tenants in Common

Tenants in common is a means of two or more co-owners owning a specified, potentially unequal percent interest in the property. This title is common for investment properties. Each tenant can sell or pass their interest to others. This title is subject to probate.

Joint Tenancy With Right of Survivorship

Joint tenancy with right of survivorship is a means of splitting equal interest in the property with two or more co-owners. When one tenant dies, the property interest is split among the surviving tenants without probate.

Tenants by the Entirety

Tenants by the entirety is similar to joint tenancy with right of survivorship except the tenants must be married and the property is owned 100% by *each* tenant. This means that creditors trying to collect an unpaid debt cannot go after the property to collect on the debt unless the debt belongs to the couple and not any individual spouse. When one spouse dies, the property goes to the surviving spouse without probate.

Community Property

Community Property is the same as tenants by the entirety except an additional benefit of the surviving spouse receiving a new stepped-up basis at market value on the date of death. This step-up in basis means that if the surviving spouse sells the property, capital gains will be based on the new stepped up value, minimizing capital gains tax.

Living Revocable Trust With Incapacity Clause

A living revocable trust allows you to put the property into any names you want and can be changed in the future. Furthermore, with an incapacity clause you can ensure property ownership transfers to another in case you become incapacitated and unable to transfer ownership but not deceased. A living trust can include the step-up in basis offered by community property in community property states. Living trusts avoid probate. The flexibility of this option and safety of the incapacity clause make this the most attractive title option. You can add other assets to the trust as well and it is advised you also construct a will to account for any remaining assets you overlook adding to the trust, but assets distributed via the will can be subject to probate. The downside is that living revocable trusts and wills require an attorney to craft them, which often costs hundreds of dollars but is generally worth the expense. A good place to find an attorney to craft a living revocable trust and will is through RocketLawyer.com.

Financial Priorities

1. Automate expense tracking and establish categorized budgets to control and predict your spending.
2. Project your finances to reveal the future impact of your spending and saving.
3. Save one month's income in an easily accessible checking account as a bank account buffer.
4. Sign up for a HSA if a High Deductible Health Plan saves you premiums or your employer contributes to your Health Savings Account. Contribute up to your employer's maximum match for free money in this HSA. If your employer's HSA match percentage is lower than their 401(k) match percentage, max out your 401(k) match before maxing out your HSA match.
5. If your employer matches contributions to your 401(k), contribute up to the maximum match for free money and invest it in low fee global market stock portfolio and domestic bond funds, increasing bond allocation as you approach retirement.
6. Save up to your expected yearly medical expenses in a HSA if you are covered by a High Deductible Health Plan for triple tax-free medical expenses.
7. Monitor and increase your credit score.
8. Pay down credit card debt in order of descending interest rate while rotating balances over 0-interest cards.
9. Earn cashback rewards on your purchases.
10. Subtract your bank account buffer from your desired emergency fund and invest twice that amount for up to four to ten months' expenses in a

Roth IRA up to the max (through a Backdoor Roth IRA or Mega Backdoor Roth IRA if necessary) then a taxable investment account for a safe, high-earning emergency fund.

11. Start saving for any short term goals such as a wedding or down payment on a house in a savings account until reaching your goal then match additional savings from income with money from your savings account and invest it in a Roth IRA up to the max (through a Backdoor Roth IRA or Mega Backdoor Roth IRA if necessary and available) then a taxable investment account until it reaches double the amount of your goal. Utilize tax loss harvesting and tax efficient asset placement to minimize your taxable investment account's taxes.
12. Set aside your excess savings—money after paying monthly debt minimums, securing employer matches, and building an emergency fund—and allocate a percentage of it equal to your target non-equity allocation multiplied by your highest effective interest rate loan divided by the expected return on bonds to pay off your highest effective interest rate loan. If all remaining debts have an effective interest rate no more than 1% above effective bond return rates and you have possible long-term needs for liquidity, you can invest in bonds to achieve your liquidity goal before directing further savings to paying down this debt.
    a. Spend less on your car by buying instead of leasing unless you expect you'll want another new car within 3 years. If you expect to have higher interest debt for the foreseeable future, finance over 5-7 years; otherwise, finance over 2-3 years.
    b. Apply for the lowest monthly payment student loan repayment plan for which you are eligible and early student loan forgiveness if eligible. Refinance with a private company if your weighted average interest rate would be lower than your federal loan rate unless you are pursuing early student loan forgiveness.
    c. **Once you know you'll be settled in a place for at least 5 years and have saved up enough savings past your emergency fund for a down payment, buy a house with the appropriate loan whether VA, USDA, Conventional, or FHA. Pick a fixed rate loan unless you know you'll be in the house for less than 10 years in which case choose an ARM. When choosing fixed rate, choose a 30 year term unless you would allocate the minimum payment of a 15 year term loan towards**

paying down your mortgage according to your percent of excess savings to apply to debt in excess of a 30 year mortgage payment. Be sure to pick a suitable title for your property, which in most cases will be a living revocable trust with incapacity clause for its flexibility and added protections.

13. Buy your financial independence by saving a target percentage of your gross income minus taxes (minimum 15%) to retire by your desired date and invest it in a tax optimal manner among your HSA, IRAs, 401(k)s, and taxable investment account. Stop using HSA funds to cover medical expenses, leaving HSA funds to compound earnings without tax-drag, and save medical receipts for future tax-free HSA withdrawals.
14. If you want to invest for future pre-retirement spending instead of using all your savings to buy financial independence, invest further savings in a tax efficient manner among your Roth IRA, Roth 401(k), and taxable investment account.
15. If you are already maxing out your retirement accounts and plan to be earning more than $24,000 per year when your children go to school, it makes sense to fund up to around 188% (47% * 4 years of education) of your adjusted allowable income to a 529 plan. That will be around 0.5% of your adjusted allowable yearly income each month over 18 years, 1.2% over 10 years, or 2.7% over 5 years. If you believe you will be making less than $25,000 per year by the time your kids go to college, such as if you retire early and withdraw less than $25,000 from your retirement accounts, then you should channel that money into a taxable account instead of a 529. Any excess savings after funding your 529 should go towards investing in a taxable investment account or paying down debt.

Chapter 16 – Life Insurance

Life insurance isn't necessary until you have people who depend on you for money. It's often overlooked because no one likes to admit there is even a small chance that life can end any day. A financial plan is not complete if it leaves you worried for your loved ones if the worst were to happen. Life insurance is a means to financially protect those who depend on you in case an accident or poor health takes your life and leaves them without access to your income which was providing for their lifestyle. It's an agreement with an insurance company to pay your beneficiaries a lump sum of money if you pass away in exchange for your ongoing premium payments. The larger the lump sum you want to leave and the older or less healthy you are, the larger your premium payments will be.

How Big a Life Insurance Policy Do You Need?

A conservative approach to life insurance is to take out an insurance policy that will provide for your partner given their current standard of living for the rest of their life. We discussed in Chapter 1 – Why Do You Want Money that a 3.5% withdrawal rate or 29 (1/0.035) times yearly expenses is expected to last a lifetime when invested. Therefore, aiming to leave your partner29 times *their* expenses is a good goal. You can remove your expenses such as your portion of food expenses from this equation. You can also remove the assets you have already accumulated from the policy total. If you are paying down a house, you may want to remove your premium payments from the expenses, but add in the balance remaining on your mortgage to pay it off. If your partner will be earning their own income, it's possible to subtract that from their yearly expenses.

[Life Insurance Policy] = 29 * [Partner yearly expenses – Partner yearly income – Yearly mortgage premium] + [Mortgage balance] – [Assets accumulated]

If you have children, it's common to cover their yearly expenses through to about age 20. For a balance to last 20 years a safe withdrawal rate is 5% or

20 (1/0.05) times yearly expenses[154] and for 10 years its around 10% or 10 (1/0.1) times yearly expenses. You might also want to add in the cost of college. In 2018, the average cost of a 4-year public in-state college tuition including room and board is around $80,000.[155] After an expected 2% yearly inflation rate, this grows to around $100,000 after 10 years and $120,000 after 20 years.

[Life Insurance Policy] = 29 * [Yearly expenses for partner – Partner yearly income – Yearly mortgage premium] + [Mortgage balance]– [Assets accumulated] + 20 * [Yearly expenses for children under the age of 10] + 10 * [Yearly expenses for children ages 10-20] + $120,00 * [Number of children under the age of 10] + $100,000 * [Number of children ages 10-20]

How to Buy Life Insurance

There are two main types of life insurance: term and whole life. Term life insurance provides coverage for a set period of time, often between 10 and 30 years. Whole life insurance provides lifelong coverage and includes an investment component known as the policy's cash value. Because whole life insurance guarantees a payout, the premiums are much higher than term life insurance where the customer usually outlives the term.[156] Because life insurance is meant to cover you for the period you earn income to fund your family's living, term life insurance and its cheaper premiums are almost always the right policy. Past that term, you should have enough money where you no longer need life insurance and can avoid paying any premiums.

Reputation and financial health of a life insurance company are very important and are graded and searchable by A.M. Best Rating Services.[157] You want to work with a responsible company that pays its customers and is

[154] https://www.kitces.com/blog/adjusting-safe-withdrawal-rates-to-the-retirees-time-horizon/

[155] http://www.aie.org/pay-for-college/understand-college-costs/how-much-will-college-cost-me.cfm

[156] https://www.nerdwallet.com/blog/insurance/what-is-the-difference-between-term-whole-life-insurance/

[157] http://www.ambest.com/home/ratings.aspx

a solvent company expected to last at least as long as your term policy to ensure you don't need to open up a new policy elsewhere.

Life insurance policies are cheaper the younger you are when you buy them so you prefer to buy them young and hold on to them. You should buy the longest policy you anticipate you'll need which for many is a 30-year or 20-year term policy.

Because the amount of insurance you need goes down as you accumulate assets, you'll want to find a provider who offers policy "riders" which are shorter-term policies built into your full term policy. For example, if I need a $900,000 policy now and anticipate working for another 30-years, I might want to take out a $300,000 30-year policy with a $300,000 20-year rider and a $300,000 10-year rider. This means that my policy offers $900,000 for the first 10 years, $600,000 for the next 10 years, and $300,000 for the last 10 years. Having this decreasing payout still fits my needs as I save up money over time and will have a lower premium payment than a $900,000 30-year policy.

Finding the best life insurance provider for you requires shopping around, but I find Term Life 2 Go's website, termlife2go.com, and Policy Genius, PolicyGenius.com, to be the best rate comparison engines to get you started. I'd be sure to add Banner Life, from parent company Legal & General,[158] to your list to explore as they are known for providing great service with some of the lowest prices and are one of the few companies that offer riders.[159]

Financial Priorities

1. Automate expense tracking and establish categorized budgets to control and predict your spending.
2. Project your finances to reveal the future impact of your spending and saving.
3. Save one month's income in an easily accessible checking account as a bank account buffer.

[158] https://www.lgamerica.com/
[159] https://www.bestliferates.org/best-life-insurance-companies/

4. Sign up for a HSA if a High Deductible Health Plan saves you premiums or your employer contributes to your Health Savings Account. Contribute up to your employer's maximum match for free money in this HSA. If your employer's HSA match percentage is lower than their 401(k) match percentage, max out your 401(k) match before maxing out your HSA match.
5. If your employer matches contributions to your 401(k), contribute up to the maximum match for free money and invest it in low fee global market stock portfolio and domestic bond funds, increasing bond allocation as you approach retirement.
6. Save up to your expected yearly medical expenses in a HSA if you are covered by a High Deductible Health Plan for triple tax-free medical expenses.
7. Monitor and increase your credit score.
8. Pay down credit card debt in order of descending interest rate while rotating balances over 0-interest cards.
9. Earn cashback rewards on your purchases.
10. Subtract your bank account buffer from your desired emergency fund and invest twice that amount for up to four to ten months' expenses in a Roth IRA up to the max (through a Backdoor Roth IRA or Mega Backdoor Roth IRA if necessary) then a taxable investment account for a safe, high-earning emergency fund.
11. **If you have anyone who depends on your income, take out a term life insurance policy that's sufficient for covering their expenses for the length of time you expect they will be dependent on your income.**
12. Start saving for any short term goals such as a wedding or down payment on a house in a savings account until reaching your goal then match additional savings from income with money from your savings account and invest it in a Roth IRA up to the max (through a Backdoor Roth IRA or Mega Backdoor Roth IRA if necessary and available) then a taxable investment account until it reaches double the amount of your goal. Utilize tax loss harvesting and tax efficient asset placement to minimize your taxable investment account's taxes.
13. Set aside your excess savings—money after paying monthly debt minimums, securing employer matches, and building an emergency fund—and allocate a percentage of it equal to your target non-equity allocation multiplied by your highest effective interest rate loan divided

by the expected return on bonds to pay off your highest effective interest rate loan. If all remaining debts have an effective interest rate no more than 1% above effective bond return rates and you have possible long-term needs for liquidity, you can invest in bonds to achieve your liquidity goal before directing further savings to paying down this debt.

a. Spend less on your car by buying instead of leasing unless you expect you'll want another new car within 3 years. If you expect to have higher interest debt for the foreseeable future, finance over 5-7 years; otherwise, finance over 2-3 years.
b. Apply for the lowest monthly payment student loan repayment plan for which you are eligible and early student loan forgiveness if eligible. Refinance with a private company if your weighted average interest rate would be lower than your federal loan rate unless you are pursuing early student loan forgiveness.
c. Once you know you'll be settled in a place for at least 5 years and have saved up enough savings past your emergency fund for a down payment, buy a house with the appropriate loan whether VA, USDA, Conventional, or FHA. Pick a fixed rate loan unless you know you'll be in the house for less than 10 years in which case choose an ARM. When choosing fixed rate, choose a 30 year term unless you would allocate the minimum payment of a 15 year term loan towards paying down your mortgage according to your percent of excess savings to apply to debt in excess of a 30 year mortgage payment. Be sure to pick a suitable title for your property, which in most cases will be a living revocable trust with incapacity clause for its flexibility and added protections.

14. Buy your financial independence by saving a target percentage of your gross income minus taxes (minimum 15%) to retire by your desired date and invest it in a tax optimal manner among your HSA, IRAs, 401(k)s, and taxable investment account. Stop using HSA funds to cover medical expenses, leaving HSA funds to compound earnings without tax-drag, and save medical receipts for future tax-free HSA withdrawals.
15. If you want to invest for future pre-retirement spending instead of using all your savings to buy financial independence, invest further savings in a tax efficient manner among your Roth IRA, Roth 401(k), and taxable investment account.

16. If you are already maxing out your retirement accounts and plan to be earning more than $24,000 per year when your children go to school, it makes sense to fund up to around 188% (47% * 4 years of education) of your adjusted allowable income to a 529 plan. That will be around 0.5% of your adjusted allowable yearly income each month over 18 years, 1.2% over 10 years, or 2.7% over 5 years. If you believe you will be making less than $25,000 per year by the time your kids go to college, such as if you retire early and withdraw less than $25,000 from your retirement accounts, then you should channel that money into a taxable account instead of a 529. Any excess savings after funding your 529 should go towards investing in a taxable investment account or paying down debt.

Chapter 17 – Car Insurance

Car Insurance

Car insurance is no different from other forms of insurance: you want to buy as little of it as you can afford given a catastrophe. But it's important to keep in mind what the catastrophe can be since with car accidents they can be quite costly. Specifically, you can be sued for all your assets—minus assets that are protected in ERISA-qualified retirement accounts—and for garnished wages up to 25% of your disposable income in many states. ERISA stands for Employee Retirement Income Security Act and it prevents an employer or plan administrator from releasing your benefits to a creditor who tries to claim rights to those assets. Common ERISA plans include 401(k)s and HSAs, but protection for IRAs are determined by states and usually aren't well protected.[160] To prevent loss of your assets and having your wages garnished, you need to ensure you are insured for any foreseeable accident with ample car insurance.

- Bodily Injury Limits
  - When you are found at fault for an accident involving bodily injury, this covers your legal fees and medical expenses for the other party you injured. It is reported for example as $100,000/$300,000 where the first number is maximum the policy covers per person injured and the second number is the maximum the policy covers per accident. It's even relevant in no-fault insurance states since they do not apply when the accident occurs out of state and often has exceptions for injuries.
  - Because serious accidents can get expensive, you should take out as much bodily injury coverage as possible which is often $250,000/$500,000 in coverage. Oftentimes this additional coverage costs less than $2/month more than the common $100,000/$300,000

---

[160] http://www.nolo.com/legal-encyclopedia/can-judgment-creditors-go-after-my-retirement-accounts.html

coverage which is well worth the peace of mind in case of a costly catastrophe.

- Property Damage Limit
  - When you are found at fault for an accident involving property damage, this covers your legal fees and damage compensation for the other party's property you damaged. Sometimes it's reported as a third number along with your bodily injury limit such as $100,000 in a $250,000/$500,000/$100,000 plan.
  - I recommend opting for $100,000 as that would replace the vast majority of cars you could damage. Furthermore, policies often increase less than $1/month in cost from a low coverage amount such as $25,000 to a high coverage amount such as $100,000.
- Personal Injury Protection (PIP)
  - Medical Coverage
    - Unlike bodily injury insurance, which covers medical expenses for the party you injure, PIP covers medical expenses for you and passengers in your car without regard to fault. If an at-fault party doesn't have insurance, it will cover you in place of what would have been their bodily injury insurance. It's similar to health insurance but also covers medical expenses of others in your car who might not have adequate health insurance. It usually covers around 80-85% of such medical expenses up to a state mandated minimum limit that an insurer must offer and is a good idea to include as much of it as your insurer offers.
  - Work Loss
    - PIP covers wages lost due to inability to work after an accident, which is often not covered by health insurance plans.
    - If you are given the option to select Primary vs Excess/Coordinated, it is likely you want to choose Primary. Selecting Excess/Coordinated allows your auto insurer to only supplement lost income after your health insurer no longer supplements income. It's possible that both your auto insurer and health insurer can both pay your work loss benefit allowing you to "double dip" on the benefits.[161] Since it's not much more expensive, you should opt for Primary coverage.

---

[161] http://www.michiganautolaw.com/buying-car-insurance/coordinated-uncoordinated/

- Deductibles
  - As I mentioned for other insurance deductibles, you should choose as high of a deductible you can afford (up to your emergency fund requirement).
- Uninsured/Underinsured Motorist Bodily Injury Limits (UM/UIM)
  - In the case that another driver is at fault and they are uninsured or underinsured and do not have assets available to cover your medical expenses, or they do a hit-and-run, this insurance covers your medical expenses.[162] In some states it is paid after the PIP cap is reached[163] while in other states it's treated separate from PIP, allowing you to again "double dip" and receive payments from a PIP claim in addition to a UM/UIM claim. It's almost always appropriate to choose the same coverage as you did for your bodily injury limit to ensure you are fully covered in this case. This is the case even in Michigan, the only state that requires unlimited 100% coverage of medical expenses under PIP, because in Michigan UM/UIM is considered separate from PIP and allows for double dipping.[164]
- Comprehensive and Collision Coverage
  - Comprehensive coverage covers damage not resulting from a collision, which is what collision covers. Choose the highest deductible you can afford (up to your emergency fund requirement) for these. Also be sure you select "standard" collision coverage which will cover you whether you are at fault or not whereas "broadform" allows you coverage without paying your deductible when you're not at fault, but comes with a higher premium, and "limited" covers you only when you are not at fault. You should be able to afford your deductible but also ensure you are protected from accidents you can't afford regardless of who's at fault.
- Gap Insurance
  - Gap insurance covers the difference between what you owe on a vehicle and the value of the car at time of being totaled or stolen

---

[162] http://www.carinsurance.com/uninsured-motorist-coverage.aspx
[163] https://www.rcslawfirm.com/relationship-pip-uninsured-motorist-coverage/
[164] http://www.michiganautolaw.com/blog/2014/06/26/miles-v-state-far/

because your comprehensive and collision coverage only covers the actual value of the car at the time, which as we mentioned earlier rapidly depreciates. If this happens, you still owe the remaining balance on your loan and are expected to continue with payments to your lender as planned. Gap insurance provides you funds to pay off your lender in full.

  - In general, I do not recommend gap insurance since it's a bit costly and you already knew you could afford your monthly loan payments when you bought the car. However, if you will need a replacement car and can't bear driving one less expensive (the value of your car at time of loss) and don't have emergency funds to cover the gap, you should buy gap insurance but be sure to buy it from your insurer and not from a dealership because they tend to offer costly deals.

- Other
  - Other add-ons such as towing and labor, customized parts and equipment, and rental coverage are best left off. Look into a reputable company such as AAA if you want to pay for roadside assistance.

Umbrella Insurance

Because 13% of personal injury liability rewards are $1 million or more, you will need more coverage than the $500,000 limit your car insurance will provide.[165] To get more coverage, insurers offer umbrella insurance which is insurance that kicks in once you've exceeded coverage limits from car and homeowners insurance but your insurer will typically require the maximum bodily injury limit coverage under your car insurance and the maximum dwelling protection before selling you umbrella insurance. These policies are typically sold with million-dollar coverage increments and so you should consider $2M of coverage as a minimum. Few cases are greater than $2 million and so $2M is a reasonable target. The cost of a $2M coverage policy should be around $300-400 per year.

[165] https://www.forbes.com/sites/ashleaebeling/2012/03/05/the-1-fear-being-sued-but-shun-umbrella-insurance/#10b0422b6166

Financial Priorities

1. Automate expense tracking and establish categorized budgets to control and predict your spending.
2. Project your finances to reveal the future impact of your spending and saving.
3. Save one month's income in an easily accessible checking account as a bank account buffer.
4. Sign up for a HSA if a High Deductible Health Plan saves you premiums or your employer contributes to your Health Savings Account. Contribute up to your employer's maximum match for free money in this HSA. If your employer's HSA match percentage is lower than their 401(k) match percentage, max out your 401(k) match before maxing out your HSA match.
5. If your employer matches contributions to your 401(k), contribute up to the maximum match for free money and invest it in low fee global market stock portfolio and domestic bond funds, increasing bond allocation as you approach retirement.
6. Save up to your expected yearly medical expenses in a HSA if you are covered by a High Deductible Health Plan for triple tax-free medical expenses.
7. Monitor and increase your credit score.
8. Pay down credit card debt in order of descending interest rate while rotating balances over 0-interest cards.
9. Earn cashback rewards on your purchases.
10. Subtract your bank account buffer from your desired emergency fund and invest twice that amount for up to four to ten months' expenses in a Roth IRA up to the max (through a Backdoor Roth IRA or Mega Backdoor Roth IRA if necessary) then a taxable investment account for a safe, high-earning emergency fund.
11. If you have anyone who depends on your income, take out a term life insurance policy that's sufficient for covering their expenses for the length of time you expect they will be dependent on your income.
12. Start saving for any short term goals such as a wedding or down payment on a house in a savings account until reaching your goal then match additional savings from income with money from your savings account and invest it in a Roth IRA up to the max (through a Backdoor Roth IRA or

Mega Backdoor Roth IRA if necessary and available) then a taxable investment account until it reaches double the amount of your goal. Utilize tax loss harvesting and tax efficient asset placement to minimize your taxable investment account's taxes.

13. Set aside your excess savings—money after paying monthly debt minimums, securing employer matches, and building an emergency fund—and allocate a percentage of it equal to your target non-equity allocation multiplied by your highest effective interest rate loan divided by the expected return on bonds to pay off your highest effective interest rate loan. If all remaining debts have an effective interest rate no more than 1% above effective bond return rates and you have possible long-term needs for liquidity, you can invest in bonds to achieve your liquidity goal before directing further savings to paying down this debt.
    a. Spend less on your car by buying instead of leasing unless you expect you'll want another new car within 3 years. If you expect to have higher interest debt for the foreseeable future, finance over 5-7 years; otherwise, finance over 2-3 years.
        i. **Take out a minimal necessary amount of collision and comprehensive car insurance but the maximum amount of bodily injury, personal injury protection, and uninsured/underinsured motorist bodily injury insurance to cover you in case of a very expensive catastrophe. Add $2 million of umbrella insurance coverage to ensure your assets and wages are protected for reasonably common personal injury award amounts.**
    b. Apply for the lowest monthly payment student loan repayment plan for which you are eligible and early student loan forgiveness if eligible. Refinance with a private company if your weighted average interest rate would be lower than your federal loan rate unless you are pursuing early student loan forgiveness.
    c. Once you know you'll be settled in a place for at least 5 years and have saved up enough savings past your emergency fund for a down payment, buy a house with the appropriate loan whether VA, USDA, Conventional, or FHA. Pick a fixed rate loan unless you know you'll be in the house for less than 10 years in which case choose an ARM. When choosing fixed rate, choose a 30 year term unless you would allocate the minimum payment of a 15 year term loan towards paying

down your mortgage according to your percent of excess savings to apply to debt in excess of a 30 year mortgage payment. Be sure to pick a suitable title for your property, which in most cases will be a living revocable trust with incapacity clause for its flexibility and added protections.

14. Buy your financial independence by saving a target percentage of your gross income minus taxes (minimum 15%) to retire by your desired date and invest it in a tax optimal manner among your HSA, IRAs, 401(k)s, and taxable investment account. Stop using HSA funds to cover medical expenses, leaving HSA funds to compound earnings without tax-drag, and save medical receipts for future tax-free HSA withdrawals.
15. If you want to invest for future pre-retirement spending instead of using all your savings to buy financial independence, invest further savings in a tax efficient manner among your Roth IRA, Roth 401(k), and taxable investment account.
16. If you are already maxing out your retirement accounts and plan to be earning more than $24,000 per year when your children go to school, it makes sense to fund up to around 188% (47% * 4 years of education) of your adjusted allowable income to a 529 plan. That will be around 0.5% of your adjusted allowable yearly income each month over 18 years, 1.2% over 10 years, or 2.7% over 5 years. If you believe you will be making less than $25,000 per year by the time your kids go to college, such as if you retire early and withdraw less than $25,000 from your retirement accounts, then you should channel that money into a taxable account instead of a 529. Any excess savings after funding your 529 should go towards investing in a taxable investment account or paying down debt.

Chapter 18 – Homeowners and Renters Insurance

Homeowners insurance is another case where you want to take out as little insurance as necessary but you also want to make sure you have enough to cover the cost of replacing your entire house in case of a catastrophe. The protections outlined below also apply to renters insurance, but with renter's insurance dwelling and structures protection isn't included since you do not own the property. Instead, with renter's insurance you are looking to cover your possessions, protect yourself from liability, and cover additional living expenses in case your rental becomes unsuitable for living in.

- Home Protection
  - Dwelling protection
    - Dwelling protection covers the home you live in and other attached structures such as an attached garage, porch, deck, or patio.
    - You want to be sure your policy covers home replacement cost (RC) and not actual cash value (ACV). If your home policy covers repairs strictly on an ACV basis, that means they'll take the items' value at the time of purchase and subtract the amount they've depreciated since. The replacement cost is the amount necessary to replace damaged or stolen belongings with new ones. Unlike actual cash value, replacement cost doesn't take depreciation into account.[166]
    - Types of protection
      - Guaranteed Replacement Coverage: This is the most comprehensive homeowner's insurance coverage. If your home is heavily damaged or destroyed, your insurance will pay for the entire cost of repairing and/or rebuilding no matter what your insurance limit. This type of coverage is no longer readily available.
      - Extended Replacement Coverage: This type of coverage is the most comprehensive of the widely available

[166] https://www.esurance.com/info/homeowners/replacement-cost-vs-actual-cost-value

plans. Extended replacement coverage will cover repairs up to the policy amount, but will, depending on the replacement percentage you select, cover an additional 20% – 200% of the policy amount for a covered claim. This additional coverage can pick up some of the extra cost if your repairs exceed your policy coverage amount. This coverage is best suited for homes in areas with common natural disasters that wipe out large areas and push up the demand and cost for new construction considerably (often up to 25%). However, this extra coverage isn't necessary for homeowners not in areas prone to natural disasters such as hurricanes and tornados if you accurately estimate replacement coverage and update it regularly.

- Replacement Coverage: This coverage will pay for the cost of rebuilding your home up to the policy amount. Most insurers offer "inflation-guard endorsement" that automatically adjusts dwelling coverage each year based on inflation or increases in construction costs which can help update your replacement coverage over time automatically for you. This is usually the optimal coverage, but be sure to sign up for "inflation-guard endorsement" or update your coverage yearly.
- Actual Cash Value Replacement Coverage: This type of coverage will pay for the actual original cash value of the damaged portions of your home. This type of coverage will generally not cover the entire current cost of fixing your home. This is not recommended and is typically only offered when buildings are very old and are not well taken care of or updated.

▪ Home replacement cost can be a lot more than the cash value of your home. It costs more for contractors to demolish and haul out the remains then build the home with brand new materials. It is advised you estimate your home replacement cost with an estimator like the free Building Cost Calculators tool at http://www.building-cost.net.[167] It takes about 30 minutes to fill out their survey. If it comes back with a number that far exceeds

[167] http://www.building-cost.net

your expectations, be sure to review the square footages and qualities you've entered as they can drastically change the estimate. It is not uncommon for replacement costs to be around 30%+ higher than the market value of your home.

- Other structures protection
  - This covers structures not attached to your dwelling such as detached garages, pools, sheds, gazebos, guest houses, barns, fences, driveways, sidewalks, and retaining walls after your deductible and up to a protection limit. Many insurers include a limit of 10% of your dwelling protection into your policy without an option to remove it. Unattached buildings often are insured for replacement cost whereas other structures such as driveways, fences, and retaining walls are often insured for actual cash value.[168] It's good to ensure your protection is high enough to cover your other structures.
- Personal property protection
  - This covers your possessions such as furniture, electronics, appliances, and jewelry whether they are in your house or elsewhere in the case of damage or theft, but typically not lost items, after your deductible and up to a protection limit. Your policy typically will have sub-limits for certain categories of property such as jewelry. You may benefit from "scheduling" certain items, which means purchasing separate coverage to protect particular high value items such as jewelry, art, or musical instruments.[169]
  - Insurers typically offer you the option to select 40%-75% of your dwelling protection for personal property protection. Be sure to take out enough insurance to cover the possessions you cannot live without. Most people can do just fine with 40% of dwelling protection set aside for personal property protection.
- Additional living expense (ALE) coverage
  - This covers your additional living expenses such as meal expenses in excess of typical meal expenses, storage fees,

---

[168] http://www.gaudette-insurance.com/Blog/bid/104789/Taking-The-Mystery-Out-of-Other-Structures-Property-Coverage

[169] https://www.allstate.com/tools-and-resources/insurance-basics/personal-property-coverage.aspx

mileage, pet boarding, laundry, and utilities for up to 12 months (24 months in California) if you temporarily need a place to stay after a covered incident.[170]

- Insurers typically offer you the option to select a limit of up to 10%-30% of your dwelling protection for additional living expenses. Typically 10% will cover your additional expenses for 12 months.

  - Water backup coverage
    - This is different from flood protection. Water must come up from the ground to damage your home for this coverage to kick in and it covers past a deductible up to a selected limit of coverage. Consider the value of necessary items you store in your basement when selecting a dollar amount of coverage. A $5,000limitis common for unfinished basements and a $10,000limit is common for finished basements.
  - Roof surfaces protection
    - Since roofs need to be replaced regularly based upon its material, insurers will often only pay for a percentage of the cost of replacement depending on how old the roof is and the material it is made out of.
- Liability protection
  - Family liability protection
    - Family liability protection covers bodily injury or property damage that happens to others as a result of your actions or negligence. Examples include not de-icing driveways in winter or not fixing a broken porch step, but it also includes non-auto related injuries you cause to others outside of your home, such as at the park.
    - Family liability protection should be set as high as possible or at least as high as required for umbrella insurance. Most policies come with a base $100,000 family liability protection, but insurers usually offer up to $500,000.
  - Guest medical protection

[170] http://www.insurance.com/home-and-renters-insurance/natural-disasters/additional-living-expenses.html

            - Guest medical protection covers injuries that happen to non-resident guests while on your property. Negligence does not need to be proven for this coverage to kick in and you won't need to pay a deductible for this coverage. You may want to have $1,000 in coverage to ensure coverage for ambulance expenses and small injuries; otherwise, your guests' health insurance should cover them.
- Deductibles
    - Wind and hail deductible
        - This is the amount you are responsible to pay for wind and hail damage before your policy kicks in. To save premium costs you should set this to be as high as you can afford to pay (your emergency fund requirement).
    - All other peril deductible
        - This is the amount you are responsible to pay for non-wind, non-hail damage before your policy kicks in. To save premium costs you should set this to be as high as you can afford to pay (your emergency fund requirement).

Financial Priorities

1. Automate expense tracking and establish categorized budgets to control and predict your spending.
2. Project your finances to reveal the future impact of your spending and saving.
3. Save one month's income in an easily accessible checking account as a bank account buffer.
4. Sign up for a HSA if a High Deductible Health Plan saves you premiums or your employer contributes to your Health Savings Account. Contribute up to your employer's maximum match for free money in this HSA. If your employer's HSA match percentage is lower than their 401(k) match percentage, max out your 401(k) match before maxing out your HSA match.
5. If your employer matches contributions to your 401(k), contribute up to the maximum match for free money and invest it in low fee global market stock portfolio and domestic bond funds, increasing bond allocation as you approach retirement.

6. Save up to your expected yearly medical expenses in a HSA if you are covered by a High Deductible Health Plan for triple tax-free medical expenses.
7. Monitor and increase your credit score.
8. Pay down credit card debt in order of descending interest rate while rotating balances over 0-interest cards.
9. Earn cashback rewards on your purchases.
10. Subtract your bank account buffer from your desired emergency fund and invest twice that amount for up to four to ten months' expenses in a Roth IRA up to the max (through a Backdoor Roth IRA or Mega Backdoor Roth IRA if necessary) then a taxable investment account for a safe, high-earning emergency fund.
11. If you have anyone who depends on your income, take out a term life insurance policy that's sufficient for covering their expenses for the length of time you expect they will be dependent on your income.
12. Start saving for any short term goals such as a wedding or down payment on a house in a savings account until reaching your goal then match additional savings from income with money from your savings account and invest it in a Roth IRA up to the max (through a Backdoor Roth IRA or Mega Backdoor Roth IRA if necessary and available) then a taxable investment account until it reaches double the amount of your goal. Utilize tax loss harvesting and tax efficient asset placement to minimize your taxable investment account's taxes.
13. Set aside your excess savings—money after paying monthly debt minimums, securing employer matches, and building an emergency fund—and allocate a percentage of it equal to your target non-equity allocation multiplied by your highest effective interest rate loan divided by the expected return on bonds to pay off your highest effective interest rate loan. If all remaining debts have an effective interest rate no more than 1% above effective bond return rates and you have possible long-term needs for liquidity, you can invest in bonds to achieve your liquidity goal before directing further savings to paying down this debt.
    a. Spend less on your car by buying instead of leasing unless you expect you'll want another new car within 3 years. If you expect to have higher interest debt for the foreseeable future, finance over 5-7 years; otherwise, finance over 2-3 years.

i. Take out a minimal necessary amount of collision and comprehensive car insurance but the maximum amount of bodily injury, personal injury protection, and uninsured/underinsured motorist bodily injury insurance to cover you in case of a very expensive catastrophe. Add $2 million of umbrella insurance coverage to ensure your assets and wages are protected for reasonably common personal injury award amounts.

b. Apply for the lowest monthly payment student loan repayment plan for which you are eligible and early student loan forgiveness if eligible. Refinance with a private company if your weighted average interest rate would be lower than your federal loan rate unless you are pursuing early student loan forgiveness.

c. Once you know you'll be settled in a place for at least 5 years and have saved up enough savings past your emergency fund for a down payment, buy a house with the appropriate loan whether VA, USDA, Conventional, or FHA. Pick a fixed rate loan unless you know you'll be in the house for less than 10 years in which case choose an ARM. When choosing fixed rate, choose a 30 year term unless you would allocate the minimum payment of a 15 year term loan towards paying down your mortgage according to your percent of excess savings to apply to debt in excess of a 30 year mortgage payment. Be sure to pick a suitable title for your property, which in most cases will be a living revocable trust with incapacity clause for its flexibility and added protections.

i. Take out enough dwelling protection in homeowners insurance to cover full replacement cost of your house, other structures, and valuable personal property you cannot do without. Take out enough liability insurance as necessary to qualify you for umbrella insurance coverage. Keep your deductibles set at or close to your security fund requirement to minimize premium payments.

14. Buy your financial independence by saving a target percentage of your gross income minus taxes (minimum 15%) to retire by your desired date and invest it in a tax optimal manner among your HSA, IRAs, 401(k)s, and taxable investment account. Stop using HSA funds to cover medical expenses, leaving HSA funds to compound earnings without tax-drag, and save medical receipts for future tax-free HSA withdrawals.

15. If you want to invest for future pre-retirement spending instead of using all your savings to buy financial independence, invest further savings in a tax efficient manner among your Roth IRA, Roth 401(k), and taxable investment account.
16. If you are already maxing out your retirement accounts and plan to be earning more than $24,000 per year when your children go to school, it makes sense to fund up to around 188% (47% * 4 years of education) of your adjusted allowable income to a 529 plan. That will be around 0.5% of your adjusted allowable yearly income each month over 18 years, 1.2% over 10 years, or 2.7% over 5 years. If you believe you will be making less than $25,000 per year by the time your kids go to college, such as if you retire early and withdraw less than $25,000 from your retirement accounts, then you should channel that money into a taxable account instead of a 529. Any excess savings after funding your 529 should go towards investing in a taxable investment account or paying down debt.

Chapter 19 – Taxes

Withholding Allowances

Your employer withholds taxes from your paycheck to pay the IRS the taxes you owe on your income. You can control how much your employer withholds by claiming "allowances" on a form W-4,[171] which you file with your employer. The more allowances you claim, the less money your employer will withhold from your paycheck. You want to claim enough allowances to ensure you won't get a tax refund, but not so many that you owe many thousands of dollars after filing your taxes.

Why do you want to ensure you won't get a tax refund? A tax refund is nothing more than the IRS refunding you because you *paid them too much* the previous year. You'd rather get that money throughout the previous year when you can be using it to pay down debt or invest and earn interest. However, if you claim too many allowances, you might owe more money than you have available to pay come tax time next year and you'll need to setup a payment plan with the IRS. Furthermore, if you claim so many allowances that you pay less than 90% of the taxes you owe for the year, you could be charged an underpayment penalty of $500. At first I recommend following the W-4 instructions to claim allowances and if you get a federal or state tax refund, increase your federal or state allowances by 1 for the next year then repeat until you owe money at tax time.[172]

Tax Deductions and Credits

Tax Deductions

Tax deductions reduce your taxable income (known as "Adjusted Gross Income" or "AGI") and therefore reduce the amount of income subject to your marginal tax rate. There are two ways to take tax deductions: the standard deduction vs itemized deductions. The standard deduction is a

[171] https://www.irs.gov/pub/irs-pdf/fw4.pdf
[172] https://www.irs.gov/publications/p17/ch04.html#en_US_2016_publink100032429

fixed amount the IRS determines you can deduct from your taxes, which in 2018 is $12,000 for single or married filing separately filers, $18,000 for heads of household, and $24,000 when married filing jointly. You can choose instead of taking the standard deduction to take itemized deductions, which you would only do if your itemized deductions were greater than your standard deduction.

Itemized deductions are how you reduce your taxable income using "items" such as student loan interest, mortgage interest, property taxes, charitable contributions, etc. While Traditional 401(k) and IRA contributions do lower your adjusted gross income, they do so "above the line," meaning they reduce your AGI before considering standard or itemized deductions and don't count towards itemized deductions. As such most people don't reach the $12,000+ threshold necessary to benefit from itemizing deductions and instead benefit from subtracting their Traditional 401(k) and IRA contributions and an additional $12,000+ standard deduction from their income to calculate their AGI. Note that in Chapter 8 – Emergency Funds, Short-Term Goals, IRAs, and Taxable Accounts, we mentioned that the government determines your eligibility for IRA contributions and related tax deductibility based on "*Modified* Adjusted Gross Income" or "MAGI," which differs from AGI in that it takes your AGI and adds back these standard and itemized deductions and even your Traditional IRA contributions.

Tax Credits

Unlike tax deductions, tax credits directly reduce the amount of tax you owe rather than reducing your taxable income. Therefore, rather than saving a percentage equal to your marginal tax rate on deductions, you save 100% of your tax credit. A few common tax credits include the Earned Income Tax Credit, the Child Tax Credit, and American Opportunity Tax Credit.

- Earned Income Tax Credit
  - You can qualify for a tax credit of up to $6,444 if you are working for a modest income and meet the following qualifications[173]:

[173] https://www.irs.gov/credits-deductions/individuals/earned-income-tax-credit/eitc-earned-income-tax-credit-questions-and-answers

- You, your spouse (if you file a joint return), and all others listed on Schedule EIC, must have a social security number that is valid for employment and is issued before the due date of the return including extensions.
- You must have earned income from working for someone else or owning or running a farm or business.
- Your filing status cannot be married filing separately.
- You must be a U.S. citizen or resident alien all year.
- You cannot be a qualifying child of another person.
- You cannot file Form 2555 or Form 2555 EZ (related to foreign earned income)
- You must be below the earned income, AGI and investment income limits as outlined below for 2018
  - Earned Income and AGI must be below[174]:

If filing...	Qualifying Children Claimed			
	Zero	**One**	**Two**	**Three or more**
Single, Head of Household or Widowed	$15,310	$40,402	$45,898	$49,298
Married Filing Jointly	$21,000	$46,102	$51,598	$54,998

  - Investment income must be below $3,400.
- And you must meet one of the following:
  - Have a qualifying child (see who is a qualifying child below)
  - If you do not have a qualifying child, you must:
    - be at least age 25 but under 65 at the end of the year,
    - live in the United States for more than half the year, and
    - not qualify as a dependent of another person.

- Child Tax Credit
  - You can qualify for a tax credit of up to $2,000 per child if the child has the following qualifications[175]:

[174] https://www.irs.gov/credits-deductions/individuals/earned-income-tax-credit/eitc-income-limits-maximum-credit-amounts-next-year
[175] https://www.irs.gov/pub/irs-pdf/p972.pdf

- Is your son, daughter, stepchild, foster child, brother, sister, stepbrother, stepsister, half brother, half sister, or a descendant of any of them (for example, your grandchild, niece, or nephew).
    - Was under age 17 at the end of the year (December 31).
    - Did not provide over half of his or her own support for the tax year.
    - Lived with you for more than half of the tax year.
    - Is claimed as a dependent on your return.
    - Does not file a joint return for the year (or files it only to claim a refund of withheld income tax or estimated tax paid).
    - Was a U.S. citizen, a U.S. national, or a U.S. resident alien.
    - Begins to phase out if your MAGI is above $400,000 when married filing jointly or $200,000 for all other filers.[176]
- Credit for Child and Dependent Care Expenses[177]
  - You can qualify for up to $3,000 for one dependent or $6,000 for two or more dependents based on care expenses.[178]
- Education Credits
  - American opportunity tax credit[179]
    - You can qualify for up to $2,500 per student. The amount of the credit is 100% of the first $2,000 of qualified education expenses you paid for each eligible student and 25% of the next $2,000 of qualified education expenses you paid for that student. But, if the credit pays your tax down to zero, you can have 40% of the remaining amount of the credit (up to $1,000) refunded to you.
  - Lifetime learning credit[180]
    - You can qualify for up to $2,000 for qualified education expenses paid for all eligible undergraduate, graduate, or professional degree students.
- Saver's Credit[181]

---

[176] https://www.forbes.com/sites/kellyphillipserb/2017/12/21/how-will-the-expanded-child-tax-credit-look-after-tax-reform/#4697fd374205

[177] https://www.irs.gov/credits-deductions/individuals/child-and-dependent-care-credit

[178] https://www.nolo.com/legal-encyclopedia/child-tax-credits.html

[179] https://www.irs.gov/individuals/aotc

[180] https://www.irs.gov/credits-deductions/individuals/llc

[181] https://www.irs.gov/retirement-plans/plan-participant-employee/retirement-savings-contributions-savers-credit

- o You can qualify for up to $2,000 ($4,000 if married filing jointly) based on saving in a 401(k), IRA, or ABLE account (tax-advantaged savings accounts for families with disabilities).

2018 Saver's Credit			
Credit Rate	**Married Filing Jointly**	**Head of Household**	**All Other Filers***
50% of your contribution	AGI not more than $38,000	AGI not more than $28,500	AGI not more than $19,000
20% of your contribution	$38,001 - $41,000	$28,501 - $30,750	$19,001 - $20,500
10% of your contribution	$41,001 - $63,000	$30,751 - $47,250	$20,501 - $31,500
0% of your contribution	more than $63,000	more than $47,250	more than $31,500

- Credit for the elderly (age 65 or older) or the disabled[182]
  - o You can qualify for up to $7,500 based on age and income. Any AGI or $25,000 for 2018 is ineligible.
- Adoption credit[183]
  - o You can qualify for up to $13,460 per adopted child.
- Residential energy efficient property credit (including solar energy)[184]
  - o You can qualify for up to $500 per each one-half kilowatt of capacity of the property based on.
    - qualified solar electric systems
    - qualified solar water heaters
    - qualified fuel cell property
    - qualified small wind energy property
    - qualified geothermal heat pumps
- Credit for purchasers of plug-in electric drive motor vehicles (hybrids)[185]
  - o You can qualify for up to $7,500 if you own a plug-in electric drive motor vehicle and began driving it this year.

---

[182] https://www.irs.gov/publications/p524/ar02.html
[183] https://www.irs.gov/taxtopics/tc607.html
[184] https://www.irs.gov/credits-deductions/individuals/residential-energy-efficient-property-credit
[185] https://www.irs.gov/credits-deductions/individuals/plug-in-electric-drive-vehicle-credit-section-30d

- Foreign tax credit[186]
  - If you paid or accrued foreign taxes to a foreign country or U.S. possession and are subject to U.S. tax on the same income, you may be able to take either a credit or an itemized deduction for those taxes. Typically the credit is the better option.
  - This foreign tax credit is the reason individuals in lower tax brackets favor keeping foreign investments in taxable accounts.

Filing Taxes

The best way to file your taxes is through tax software such as TurboTax. You could fill out each form yourself but this is usually more complicated and it won't ask you questions to determine if you've claimed all applicable exemptions, deductions, and credits like tax software will. You could also have a professional file your taxes, but that often costs $150-$300 and you won't have a firm grasp on your yearly financial situation like you will after using tax software to file your taxes for a few hours. However, it is useful to be familiar with a few forms even when preparing taxes with tax software.

- W-2 from your employer
  - The IRS requires your employer to report your wage, salary, and any taxes that were already withheld from your paycheck for the tax year. Your employer must make this available to you no later than January 31st following the previous tax year.
- 1099-INT (interest)
  - If you've received interest from any account such as your checking or savings account, you will be required to file this form.
- 1099-DIV (dividends) forms
  - If you've received dividends from taxable accounts, you will be required to file this form.
- 1099-B forms showing brokerage trades in stocks and bonds
  - If you sell stocks or bonds from a taxable account, you will be required to file this form to account for your capital gains.
- 1098-E showing interest paid on student loans
  - If you have student loans, you will be required to file this form to deduct your student loan interest from taxes.

---

[186] https://www.irs.gov/individuals/international-taxpayers/foreign-tax-credit

- 1098 showing interest paid on mortgage
  - If you have a mortgage, you will be required to file this form to deduct your mortgage interest and property taxes from taxes.
- Documentation showing deductions like charitable contributions, medical expenses, and IRA contributions
  - Charitable contributions require receipts of contribution when totaling at least $250 per person.

Financial Priorities

1. Automate expense tracking and establish categorized budgets to control and predict your spending.
2. Project your finances to reveal the future impact of your spending and saving.
3. Save one month's income in an easily accessible checking account as a bank account buffer.
4. Sign up for a HSA if a High Deductible Health Plan saves you premiums or your employer contributes to your Health Savings Account. Contribute up to your employer's maximum match for free money in this HSA. If your employer's HSA match percentage is lower than their 401(k) match percentage, max out your 401(k) match before maxing out your HSA match.
5. If your employer matches contributions to your 401(k), contribute up to the maximum match for free money and invest it in low fee global market stock portfolio and domestic bond funds, increasing bond allocation as you approach retirement.
6. Save up to your expected yearly medical expenses in a HSA if you are covered by a High Deductible Health Plan for triple tax-free medical expenses.
7. Monitor and increase your credit score.
8. Pay down credit card debt in order of descending interest rate while rotating balances over 0-interest cards.
9. Earn cashback rewards on your purchases.
10. Subtract your bank account buffer from your desired emergency fund and invest twice that amount for up to four to ten months' expenses in a Roth IRA up to the max (through a Backdoor Roth IRA or Mega Backdoor

Roth IRA if necessary) then a taxable investment account for a safe, high-earning emergency fund.

11. If you have anyone who depends on your income, take out a term life insurance policy that's sufficient for covering their expenses for the length of time you expect they will be dependent on your income.
12. Start saving for any short term goals such as a wedding or down payment on a house in a savings account until reaching your goal then match additional savings from income with money from your savings account and invest it in a Roth IRA up to the max (through a Backdoor Roth IRA or Mega Backdoor Roth IRA if necessary and available) then a taxable investment account until it reaches double the amount of your goal. Utilize tax loss harvesting and tax efficient asset placement to minimize your taxable investment account's taxes.
13. Set aside your excess savings—money after paying monthly debt minimums, securing employer matches, and building an emergency fund—and allocate a percentage of it equal to your target non-equity allocation multiplied by your highest effective interest rate loan divided by the expected return on bonds to pay off your highest effective interest rate loan. If all remaining debts have an effective interest rate no more than 1% above effective bond return rates and you have possible long-term needs for liquidity, you can invest in bonds to achieve your liquidity goal before directing further savings to paying down this debt.
    a. Spend less on your car by buying instead of leasing unless you expect you'll want another new car within 3 years. If you expect to have higher interest debt for the foreseeable future, finance over 5-7 years; otherwise, finance over 2-3 years.
        i. Take out a minimal necessary amount of collision and comprehensive car insurance but the maximum amount of bodily injury, personal injury protection, and uninsured/underinsured motorist bodily injury insurance to cover you in case of a very expensive catastrophe. Add $2 million of umbrella insurance coverage to ensure your assets and wages are protected for reasonably common personal injury award amounts.
    b. Apply for the lowest monthly payment student loan repayment plan for which you are eligible and early student loan forgiveness if eligible. Refinance with a private company if your weighted average

interest rate would be lower than your federal loan rate unless you are pursuing early student loan forgiveness.

c. Once you know you'll be settled in a place for at least 5 years and have saved up enough savings past your emergency fund for a down payment, buy a house with the appropriate loan whether VA, USDA, Conventional, or FHA. Pick a fixed rate loan unless you know you'll be in the house for less than 10 years in which case choose an ARM. When choosing fixed rate, choose a 30 year term unless you would allocate the minimum payment of a 15 year term loan towards paying down your mortgage according to your percent of excess savings to apply to debt in excess of a 30 year mortgage payment. Be sure to pick a suitable title for your property, which in most cases will be a living revocable trust with incapacity clause for its flexibility and added protections.

   i. Take out enough dwelling protection in homeowners insurance to cover full replacement cost of your house, other structures, and valuable personal property you cannot do without. Take out enough liability insurance as necessary to qualify you for umbrella insurance coverage. Keep your deductibles set at or close to your security fund requirement to minimize premium payments.

14. Buy your financial independence by saving a target percentage of your gross income minus taxes (minimum 15%) to retire by your desired date and invest it in a tax optimal manner among your HSA, IRAs, 401(k)s, and taxable investment account. Stop using HSA funds to cover medical expenses, leaving HSA funds to compound earnings without tax-drag, and save medical receipts for future tax-free HSA withdrawals.

15. If you want to invest for future pre-retirement spending instead of using all your savings to buy financial independence, invest further savings in a tax efficient manner among your Roth IRA, Roth 401(k), and taxable investment account.

16. If you are already maxing out your retirement accounts and plan to be earning more than $24,000 per year when your children go to school, it makes sense to fund up to around 188% (47% * 4 years of education) of your adjusted allowable income to a 529 plan. That will be around 0.5% of your adjusted allowable yearly income each month over 18 years, 1.2% over 10 years, or 2.7% over 5 years. If you believe you will be making less than $25,000 per year by the time your kids go to college,

such as if you retire early and withdraw less than $25,000 from your retirement accounts, then you should channel that money into a taxable account instead of a 529. Any excess savings after funding your 529 should go towards investing in a taxable investment account or paying down debt.

17. **Claim the maximum number of tax allowances ensuring you still pay at least 90% of the taxes you owe to avoid a penalty and take advantage of any tax credits you are eligible for.**

Chapter 20 – Retirement Planning

As mentioned in Chapter 5 – 401(k)s a portfolio can sustain itself over 30 years when withdrawing at most 4.11% and over 60 years when withdrawing at most 3.63% and adjusting the yearly withdrawal amount for inflation to maintain a constant standard of living for the remainder of life. This calculation is known as a "safe withdrawal rate." These safe withdrawal rates are calculated as coming from no-fee, tax-free accounts and we need to consider their impact on our safe withdrawal rate.

Michael Kitces found that fees reduce the safe withdrawal rate by about 40% of the fee rather than the entirety of the fee such that a 0.25% expense ratio would reduce the safe withdrawal rate by about 0.1%.[187] This is because in the cases where the portfolio declines in value, so does the amount of the fee, whereas withdrawals continue to grow with inflation. This makes the fee have a diminishing impact relative to the withdrawals over time in the cases where the portfolio fails. If you've invested in Vanguard funds the way we suggested in Chapter 5 – 401(k)s, the fees are so small that they wouldn't decrease your safe withdrawal rate by more than 0.04%.

The impact of taxes on your safe withdrawal rate depends on your personal financial situation and should be discussed with a financial advisor, but it's possible to minimize—and for some completely eliminate—taxes with an appropriate retirement drawdown strategy.

Retirement Drawdown

The best place for your retirement funds is in roth accounts where they will never again be taxed and are not subject to required minimum distributions. While you cannot contribute to roth accounts without earned income, you can rollover funds from traditional retirement accounts into your Roth IRA, but this can trigger taxes. Your goal is to get your funds into your Roth IRA while paying as little taxes as possible. Given the standard

[187] https://www.kitces.com/blog/the-impact-of-investment-costs-on-safe-withdrawal-rates/

deduction is $12,000 for single or married filing separately filers, $18,000 for heads of household, and $24,000 when married filing jointly, you can roll that amount from traditional retirement accounts into your Roth IRA each year without paying any taxes.

But what income will you live on? This is where the low long-term capital gains taxes come in. As long as your income and capital gains don't push you out of the 0% long-term capital gains tax bracket, you can take income from your taxable investment account without paying any taxes! This means after using the standard deduction for roth conversions, single or married filing separately filers can withdraw up to $26,600 of capital gains, heads of household up to $33,700 of capital gains, and married filing jointly filers up to $53,200 of capital gains without paying any taxes![188] Keep in mind that capital gains are the gains over your initial investment (cost basis), so you can take out even more money when you include your cost basis.

Long-Term Capital Gains Rate	Single Taxpayers	Married Filing Jointly	Head of Household	Married Filing Separately
0%	Up to $38,600	Up to $77,200	Up to $51,700	Up to $38,600
15%	$38,600-$425,800	$77,200-$479,000	$51,700-$452,400	$38,600-$239,500
20%	Over $425,800	Over $479,000	Over $452,400	Over $239,500

After maxing out your tax-free roth conversions and taking enough taxable account withdrawals to cover your yearly withdrawal, if you haven't reached the top of your 0% long-term capital gains bracket you can take advantage of tax-*gain* harvesting with the remainder. Tax-gain harvesting is the opposite of tax-loss harvesting and it is advantageous for those in the

---

[188] https://www.fool.com/taxes/2017/12/22/your-guide-to-capital-gains-taxes-in-2018.aspx

0% long-term capital gains tax bracket. By selling investments in your taxable account that have gains since your initial investment and immediately buying them back, you step up your cost basis to be the amount you just bought the investment for. The sale makes your long-term capital gains subject to taxes, but as your long-term capital gains tax rate is 0%, you owe no taxes! A higher cost basis sets you up for minimizing future taxes in the case where your portfolio grows large enough to allow for yearly withdrawals larger than those allowed in the 0% long-term capital gains tax bracket or where those taxes increase in the future.

Kitces Ratcheting Rule

The emphasis of the safe withdrawal rate is on the word "safe." The truth is it is designed to work even in the worst of times and most of the time your portfolio will do much better. With a 4% withdrawal rate and a constant 60% stock allocation, only about 10% of the rolling 30-year periods from the early 1870s to the present found the retiree ending 30 years with less than their initial principal. In fact, over 2/3rds of the time the retiree finishes with more than double their initial principal! This calls for a rule to allow for increased spending when your portfolio does well while ensuring the increased spend doesn't increase the original target portfolio failure rate. This rule should allow the retiree to get used to a higher standard living when the portfolio is successful and therefore never call for spending decreases. The rule is called the "Kitces Racheting Rule." It calls for a spending increase of 10% over and above the planned inflation adjusted spend whenever your portfolio sustains a balance of 50% over the initial principal for three consecutive years and this increase can happen every three years at most. This rule "dominates" the safe withdrawal rate because it never threatens the safe withdrawal rate plan and allows for more spending during retirement.

Social Security

If you are of an eligible age, you can reduce the yearly expenses your safe withdrawal rate needs to replace by retirement income from social security or pensions. While pensions are particular to your individual situation and the future of social security can change, we can cover the basics of social security as it exists today.

To qualify for social security, you need to accumulate a certain number of "credits." In 2018 you earn 1 credit for every $1,320 you earn up to a maximum of 4 credits for the year. The number of credits you need depends on your age when you apply and the type of benefit application. No one needs more than 40 credits for any social security benefit, but in general most people must have worked for at least 10 years to qualify for social security.[189] You then can start receiving social security benefits as income as early as age 62 or as late as age 70.

The amount of your benefit depends on your average monthly income over your highest earning 35 years with zeros filled in for any of those 35 years you didn't earn income.[190] The income is adjusted or "indexed" to account for changes in average wages since the year the earnings were received.[191] Once this average monthly income is calculated, it is applied against a series of "bend points" designed to replace a higher proportion of income for low-income earners than high-income earners. In 2018 your first $895 is multiplied by 0.90, your next $896 to $5,397 is multiplied by 0.32, and your remaining average monthly income is multiplied by 0.15 that when added up make up your monthly benefit called "PIA" (primary insurance amount).[192] You are eligible to receive the PIA amount upon your normal retirement age which depends on your birth year and ranges from 65 to 67.[193] If you start taking social security benefits before your normal retirement age you will receive a PIA reduction of up to 30% less and if you delay taking social security benefits until age 70 you will receive a PIA addition of up to 32% more.[194] Typically retirees need more than their social security benefit to maintain their standard of living through retirement.

---

[189] https://faq.ssa.gov/link/portal/34011/34019/Article/3829/How-do-I-earn-Social-Security-credits-and-how-many-do-I-need-to-qualify-for-benefits
[190] https://www.aarp.org/retirement/social-security/info-2016/how-social-security-calculates-benefits.html
[191] https://www.ssa.gov/pubs/EN-05-10070.pdf
[192] https://www.ssa.gov/oact/cola/piaformula.html
[193] https://www.ssa.gov/oact/ProgData/nra.html
[194] https://www.ssa.gov/planners/retire/applying2.html

It's generally considered best to wait until age 70 to start taking social security. This is because the benefit increase is large and life expectations have greatly increased since 1983 when the current social security rules were established.[195] For a lower-earning spouse, it often makes sense to only wait until full retirement age (between 65 to 67) because at that point this lower-earning spouse then has a choice between their own benefits, or spousal or survivor benefits based on their spouse's record, whichever is higher. This spousal benefit can be taken earlier, but caps out at 50% of the higher-earning spouse's full retirement social security benefit upon your full retirement age.[196] Also, if you wait to take the spousal benefit until full retirement age, you are then allowed to switch to your own retirement benefit at a later age if that becomes higher, but if you take it earlier, you do not get this option.[197]

Financial Priorities

1. Automate expense tracking and establish categorized budgets to control and predict your spending.
2. Project your finances to reveal the future impact of your spending and saving.
3. Save one month's income in an easily accessible checking account as a bank account buffer.
4. Sign up for a HSA if a High Deductible Health Plan saves you premiums or your employer contributes to your Health Savings Account. Contribute up to your employer's maximum match for free money in this HSA. If your employer's HSA match percentage is lower than their 401(k) match percentage, max out your 401(k) match before maxing out your HSA match.
5. If your employer matches contributions to your 401(k), contribute up to the maximum match for free money and invest it in low fee global market stock portfolio and domestic bond funds, increasing bond allocation as you approach retirement.

---

[195] https://www.cnbc.com/2018/07/11/if-you-cant-wait-until-70-this-is-the-next-best-age-to-claim-social-.html

[196] https://money.usnews.com/money/personal-finance/retirement/articles/2015/03/06/how-to-maximize-social-security-with-spousal-benefits

[197] https://www.ssa.gov/planners/retire/applying6.html

6. Save up to your expected yearly medical expenses in a HSA if you are covered by a High Deductible Health Plan for triple tax-free medical expenses.
7. Monitor and increase your credit score.
8. Pay down credit card debt in order of descending interest rate while rotating balances over 0-interest cards.
9. Earn cashback rewards on your purchases.
10. Subtract your bank account buffer from your desired emergency fund and invest twice that amount for up to four to ten months' expenses in a Roth IRA up to the max (through a Backdoor Roth IRA or Mega Backdoor Roth IRA if necessary) then a taxable investment account for a safe, high-earning emergency fund.
11. If you have anyone who depends on your income, take out a term life insurance policy that's sufficient for covering their expenses for the length of time you expect they will be dependent on your income.
12. Start saving for any short term goals such as a wedding or down payment on a house in a savings account until reaching your goal then match additional savings from income with money from your savings account and invest it in a Roth IRA up to the max (through a Backdoor Roth IRA or Mega Backdoor Roth IRA if necessary and available) then a taxable investment account until it reaches double the amount of your goal. Utilize tax loss harvesting and tax efficient asset placement to minimize your taxable investment account's taxes.
13. Set aside your excess savings—money after paying monthly debt minimums, securing employer matches, and building an emergency fund—and allocate a percentage of it equal to your target non-equity allocation multiplied by your highest effective interest rate loan divided by the expected return on bonds to pay off your highest effective interest rate loan. If all remaining debts have an effective interest rate no more than 1% above effective bond return rates and you have possible long-term needs for liquidity, you can invest in bonds to achieve your liquidity goal before directing further savings to paying down this debt.
    a. Spend less on your car by buying instead of leasing unless you expect you'll want another new car within 3 years. If you expect to have higher interest debt for the foreseeable future, finance over 5-7 years; otherwise, finance over 2-3 years.
        i. Take out a minimal necessary amount of collision and comprehensive car insurance but the maximum amount of bodily

injury, personal injury protection, and uninsured/underinsured motorist bodily injury insurance to cover you in case of a very expensive catastrophe. Add $2 million of umbrella insurance coverage to ensure your assets and wages are protected for reasonably common personal injury award amounts.

b. Apply for the lowest monthly payment student loan repayment plan for which you are eligible and early student loan forgiveness if eligible. Refinance with a private company if your weighted average interest rate would be lower than your federal loan rate unless you are pursuing early student loan forgiveness.

c. Once you know you'll be settled in a place for at least 5 years and have saved up enough savings past your emergency fund for a down payment, buy a house with the appropriate loan whether VA, USDA, Conventional, or FHA. Pick a fixed rate loan unless you know you'll be in the house for less than 10 years in which case choose an ARM. When choosing fixed rate, choose a 30 year term unless you would allocate the minimum payment of a 15 year term loan towards paying down your mortgage according to your percent of excess savings to apply to debt in excess of a 30 year mortgage payment. Be sure to pick a suitable title for your property, which in most cases will be a living revocable trust with incapacity clause for its flexibility and added protections.

   i. Take out enough dwelling protection in homeowners insurance to cover full replacement cost of your house, other structures, and valuable personal property you cannot do without. Take out enough liability insurance as necessary to qualify you for umbrella insurance coverage. Keep your deductibles set at or close to your security fund requirement to minimize premium payments.

14. Buy your financial independence by saving a target percentage of your gross income minus taxes (minimum 15%) to retire by your desired date and invest it in a tax optimal manner among your HSA, IRAs, 401(k)s, and taxable investment account. Stop using HSA funds to cover medical expenses, leaving HSA funds to compound earnings without tax-drag, and save medical receipts for future tax-free HSA withdrawals.

15. If you want to invest for future pre-retirement spending instead of using all your savings to buy financial independence, invest further savings in a tax efficient manner among your Roth IRA, Roth 401(k), and taxable investment account.

16. If you are already maxing out your retirement accounts and plan to be earning more than $24,000 per year when your children go to school, it makes sense to fund up to around 188% (47% * 4 years of education) of your adjusted allowable income to a 529 plan. That will be around 0.5% of your adjusted allowable yearly income each month over 18 years, 1.2% over 10 years, or 2.7% over 5 years. If you believe you will be making less than $25,000 per year by the time your kids go to college, such as if you retire early and withdraw less than $25,000 from your retirement accounts, then you should channel that money into a taxable account instead of a 529. Any excess savings after funding your 529 should go towards investing in a taxable investment account or paying down debt.
17. Claim the maximum number of tax allowances ensuring you still pay at least 90% of the taxes you owe to avoid a penalty and take advantage of any tax credits you are eligible for.
18. **Determine your safe withdrawal rate based upon your failure rate comfort level and a 40% starting stock allocation that rises 0.4% per month until reaching 100% stocks. Use tax-free roth conversions, taxable investment withdrawals, and tax-gain harvesting to minimize taxes. Ratchet up spending by 10% once every 3 consecutive years that your portfolio sustains a balance of 50% more than your initial retirement principal. Delay taking social security for as long as possible unless you're taking spousal social security benefits.**

Chapter 21 – Summary

Throughout our journey through Money Smartly we have built your tools to budget, project your finances into the future, invest in a tax-efficient and liquid manner, build a safe yet high growth emergency fund, pay off debt, insure yourself against catastrophe, and plan your retirement. Due to the power of compounding net worth, doing these smartly can literally earn the average American hundreds of thousands of dollars they otherwise wouldn't see. It's sad that personal finance education isn't required in our school system. While the optimal financial practices aren't necessarily elementary, after being introduced to them, most find them far less complex than they would have imagined. Hopefully after reading this book, you feel comfortable managing your own money and confident in why you are managing it the way you are.

Made in United States
Cleveland, OH
05 November 2026

47601851R00112